Cinetek series

The Emperor's Naked Army Marches On

o

Yukiyukite shingun

Jeffrey Ruoff and Kenneth Ruoff

FLICKS
BOOKS

A CIP catalogue record for this book is available from the British Library.

ISBN 0 948911 05 0

First published in 1998 by

Flicks Books
29 Bradford Road
Trowbridge
Wiltshire BA14 9AN
England
tel   +44 1225 767728
fax +44 1225 760418

© Jeffrey Ruoff and Kenneth Ruoff, 1998

All rights reserved. No part of this publication may be reproduced, stored in a retrieval system or transmitted in any form or by any means: electronic, electrostatic, magnetic tape, mechanical, photocopying, recording or otherwise, without prior permission in writing from the publishers.

Printed and bound in Great Britain by Antony Rowe Ltd.

Contents

Acknowledgements	iv
Cast	vi
List of scenes	1
The memory of war	2
Hara Kazuo's biography and filmography	3
In the name of the Emperor: the historical context	9
The making of *The Emperor's Naked Army Marches On*	14
Character analysis: Okuzaki as action hero	19
Narrative analysis: anatomy of an investigation	25
Reception history: Japanese memories of the war	38
Notes	45
Credits	53
Index	54

Acknowledgements

We would like to thank Hara Kazuo and Kobayashi Sachiko for freely answering our questions and lending us copies of their films. (Please note that all Japanese names appear in the text with the family name first.) We are grateful to Amy Petersen, whose editorial skills significantly improved the manuscript. Sections of this work were presented in December 1994 to the Political Science Research Group in the Faculty of Law at Hokkaido University. Our thanks to Faculty members there for their helpful suggestions. Enid Ruoff also provided useful comments on an earlier version of the manuscript. This book is partly based on our co-authored articles, "Japan's Outlaw Filmmaker: An Interview with Hara Kazuo" and "Filming at the Margins: The Documentaries of Hara Kazuo", in *Iris: A Journal of Theory on Image and Sound* 16 (spring 1993): 103-126.

I like to make dramatic movies. I feel strongly about this, more than other directors. I love Hollywood action films, and I wanted Okuzaki to act like an action star. I want to make action documentary films. (Hara Kazuo)

Cast

(In order of appearance)

Okuzaki Kenzō, ex-Private, 36th Engineering Corps
Okuzaki Shizumi, Okuzaki Kenzō's wife
Mr Otagaki, groom
Miss Sano, bride
Chief of Surveillance, Hyogo Police
Yamada Kichitarō, ex-Sergeant
Shimamoto Iseko, mother of Private Shimamoto Masayuki
Takami Minoru, ex-Sergeant, execution squad member
Seo Yukio, ex-Sergeant, execution squad member
Sakimoto Rinko, sister of executed Private Yoshizawa
Nomura Toshiya, brother of executed Private Nomura Jinpei
Aikawa Riichi, ex-Corporal, execution squad member
Hara Toshio, ex-Sergeant, execution squad member
Hamaguchi Masaichi, ex-Sergeant and medic, execution squad member
Maruyama Tarō, ex-Sergeant and doctor, execution squad witness
Kojima Shichirō, ex-Sergeant
Kuwata Hiroshi, teacher, accomplice of Okuzaki
Koshimizu Masao, ex-Captain, executioner
Ōshima Eizaburo, anarchist, accomplice of Okuzaki

The Emperor's Naked Army Marches On

List of scenes

1. Okuzaki Kenzō acts as a go-between at a wedding in Yabu.
2. Intertitles announce Okuzaki's convictions, and the title of the film appears.
3. Okuzaki phones and then meets with the Chief of Surveillance, Hyogo Police.
4. Okuzaki visits Yamada Kichitarō in a Fukaya hospital.
5. Okuzaki protests against the Shōwa Emperor's birthday in Tokyo.
6. Okuzaki lectures a group of lawyers about his actions and trials.
7. Okuzaki tries to visit Kobe Prison to measure a cell.
8. Okuzaki prays with Shimamoto Iseko over her dead son in Hiroshima.
9. Okuzaki prays for the soul of Private Yamazaki in Hyogo.
10. Okuzaki prays for the soul of Sergeant Tanaka in Nantan, Hyogo.
11. Okuzaki ambushes Takami Minoru in his home in Yagake, Okayama.
12. Okuzaki confronts Seo Yukio in his home in Hakuta, Shimane.
13. Sakimoto Rinko, Private Yoshizawa's sister, speaks of her brother's death.
14. Okuzaki, Sakimoto and Nomura Toshiya interview Aikawa Riichi.
15. Okuzaki and relatives confront Hara Toshio in Iwasa, Yamanashi.
16. Okuzaki and relatives ambush ex-medic Hamaguchi Masaichi in Nagata, Kobe.
17. Okuzaki and relatives interview ex-doctor Maruyama Tarō in Hyogo.
18. Sakimoto and Nomura visit a graveyard together.

2 · *The Emperor's Naked Army Marches On*

19 Okuzaki discusses the executions on the phone with Kojima Shichirō.
20 Okuzaki recruits his wife, Shizumi, and Kuwata Hiroshi to accompany him.
21 Okuzaki and his associates ambush Koshimizu Masao.
22 Okuzaki and his associates confront Seo Yukio again.
23 Okuzaki and his associates ambush Takami Minoru again.
24 Okuzaki recruits Ōshima Eizaburo to investigate the death of Hashimoto.
25 Okuzaki and his associates confront Yamada Kichitarō at home.
26 Okuzaki, with Shizumi, discusses the use of violence in front of a hospital.
27 Okuzaki takes a ferry to the cemetery to pray.
28 An intertitle details the New Guinea trip, and headlines describe Okuzaki's attack.
29 Okuzaki Shizumi publicises her husband's case.
30 Intertitles announce the results of the hearing. Credits.

* * *

The memory of war

In 1987, a highly original and controversial film, *Yukiyukite shingun* (*The Emperor's Naked Army Marches On*), premièred in Tokyo. Directed by Hara Kazuo, this provocative work traces Okuzaki Kenzō's efforts to chronicle atrocities, including murder and cannibalism, committed by Japanese soldiers in occupied New Guinea. Okuzaki, a veteran of the Pacific War, denounces the Shōwa Emperor (Hirohito) throughout the film, thus challenging one of the strongest taboos in Japan. Not since Ichikawa Kon's *Nobi* (*Fires on the Plains*, 1959) has a Japanese film dealt so frankly with the issues of cannibalism, the abuse of soldiers by their officers, and desertion in the Imperial Army during the Second World War. With the exception of *Nippon no higeki* (*The Japanese Tragedy*, 1946), an historical documentary banned by American occupation authorities shortly after its release because it advocated that the Emperor be put on trial as a war criminal, no Japanese film has ever confronted the issue of the Emperor's war responsibility so relentlessly.[1]

The *Emperor's Naked Army Marches On* focuses on a man who struggles single-handedly to challenge the postwar political Establishment. While Japanese intellectuals debated the relevance of the emperor system and the morality of individual and collective responsibility, Okuzaki Kenzō took direct action. He is infamous in Japan for having slung *pachinko* balls (small marbles) at the Emperor in front of the Imperial Palace in 1969. In *The Emperor's Naked Army Marches On*, Okuzaki continues his violent political activities. This haunting work was not Hara's first film, nor his first brush with controversy: "From my viewpoint, a documentary should explore things that people don't want explored, bring things out of the closet, to examine why people want to hide certain things".[2] Like the director Imamura Shōhei in *Nippon sengoshi: Madamu Onboro no seikatsu* (*History of Japan as Told by a Bar Hostess*, 1970) and *Karayuki-san* (*Karayuki-san, the Making of a Prostitute*, 1973), Hara portrays contemporary Japanese society and history through the lives of radicals, outcasts and marginals. Fittingly, Hara's *The Emperor's Naked Army Marches On* – the story of an eccentric veteran who seeks to avenge the injustices of the war – is the most significant documentary film produced in Japan in the 53 years since the end of the Pacific War.

Hara Kazuo's biography and filmography

Hara Kazuo's life and work have been shaped by witnessing the protest movements of the late-1960s and early 1970s:

> I did not go to college. I did not participate in the demonstrations. I was on the outside looking in...The sense of failure among those who participated was strong. But I was not directly involved, so I don't have this feeling of failure; I was always...on the outside, thinking to myself, 'how wonderful.' The 60s and 70s continue to shine in my mind.[3]

In keeping with his background, Hara makes films that attack mainstream society, and does so from the perspective of an outsider:

> My outlaw complex is very strong. I don't feel that I am in the middle of society. I am in the lower part. Those

people on the bottom disdain those people in the mainstream. A movie director from the 'bottom' does not make movies that portray mainstream society nicely. I make bitter films.[4]

Hara's anti-Establishment stance emerges clearly from his choice of subjects. The main characters in his first three documentaries – a disabled poet; a radical feminist; and a stubborn anti-emperorist veteran of Japan's campaign in New Guinea – are marginal individuals who call into question conventional values. Hara's most recent film focuses on the famous left-wing essayist, Inoue Mitsuharu, who not only wrote stories, but also, as the film shows, invented a fictional personal history.

* * *

Hara Kazuo was born in 1945, the most turbulent year in Japan's 20th-century history. The country's Fifteen Years War to dominate Asia, between 1931 and 1945, ended in catastrophic defeat and foreign occupation. The period after the surrender was miserable for most Japanese, characterised by widespread hunger and even starvation. Hara never saw his father's face, and his family was poor. He attended public schools. (The educational system had been reformed during the occupation era [1945-52] to extend opportunities and stress the teaching of democracy.) After graduating from secondary school, Hara went to the capital to attend the Tōkyō Shashin Senmon Gakkō (Tokyo Academy of Photography). To support himself, he worked part-time in a school for children with disabilities, and found in the youngsters subjects for his art. In 1969, he exhibited his collected photographs of these children at the Nikon Salon in the Ginza area of Tokyo. The show was titled "Baka ni sunna" ("Don't Make Fun of Them"). At the exhibition he met his present wife, Kobayashi Sachiko.

It was during these years that social movements rocked Japan. Students took to the streets to protest about matters as global as American imperialism and as local as imperialism in the Japanese family. Workers had their own diverse objections to the status quo, and so they joined the students in the streets. Feminists demanded fuller participation of women in Japanese society. These movements were united by a willingness to challenge accepted values. This deeply influenced Hara: "[T]here was a movement in the 60s and 70s to attack taboos, and I feel the need to live up to that. This sense of the freedom to break taboos, this emancipation, helped me to start making films."[5] In 1971, Hara founded Shissō Productions with Kobayashi Sachiko. She has produced all his films, and Hara speaks of the works as collaborations.

Hara's first documentary, like his exhibition of photographs, focuses on the disabled. *Sayonara CP* (*Goodbye CP*, 1972), made in collaboration with a group of individuals with cerebral palsy, shocked audiences with its stark images of physical disability. In response, one critic, Saitō Masaharu, accused Hara of sadism. Quite deliberately, *Goodbye CP* challenges taboos about representations of disabled people, and, in particular, the shame associated with physical difference. The protagonist Yokota Hiroshi proudly displays his naked body on a street in central Yokohama. Hara noted in an interview: "It is difficult to look at handicapped people's bodies...so that's what I wanted to show".[6] Yokota asserts his right to appear different, to crawl around town on all fours, rather than use a wheelchair. The director encourages the disabled to speak for themselves as participants, rather than as victims; as Yokota matter-of-factly states: "Pity I can do without". *Goodbye CP* does not allow a facile empathy with the plight of people with disabilities, but rather forces viewers to confront their own fears and misgivings.

As would be the case with all of Hara's films, the making of *Goodbye CP* generated considerable controversy. Yokota's wife, Yoshiko, also disabled, argues on camera that the filming is undermining their attempts to join mainstream society. Characteristically, Hara includes the ensuing argument between Yokota and his wife in the documentary itself, forcing debate about the process and the ethics of representation. Yoshiko threatens divorce if her husband continues his participation, contending that Hara is portraying him as a "freak". Hearing of Yokota's intention to drop out of the project, his peers show up at the apartment and encourage him, as the man of the house, to stand up to his wife. A harsh battle ensues between Yoshiko and her husband in which she also lashes out at the filmmaker, crying: "This is an invasion of the home".

Hara's reflexive approach intentionally opens up questions of documentary practice for subjects and viewers. In what would become a pattern with his films, individuals involved penned their memories of the production and their interpretations of the result.[7] A very low-budget feature,[8] shot in black-and-white with non-synchronous location sound, *Goodbye CP* had little impact on the film world, but played a crucial role in redefining the ways in which people with disabilities were treated and represented in Japan. The director was repeatedly invited to speak at conferences of social workers and health-care providers. Hara and Kobayashi separately authored articles calling for changes in the treatment of the handicapped, and criticising state interference in the question of whether disabled individuals should bear children.[9]

Hara's second film was another low-budget production, costing about five million yen (approximately $40 000 at 120 yen to the dollar). *Kyokushiteki erosu koiuta 1974* (*Extreme Private Eros: Love Song 1974*, 1974) explores issues of intimate family relationships, privacy and gender roles. These subjects also became topical in American documentaries in the 1970s. Craig Gilbert's twelve-episode public television series, *An American Family* (1973), for example, focuses on the controversial topics of divorce and sexuality.[10] In *Extreme Private Eros: Love Song 1974*, Hara follows the activities of his estranged wife, Takeda Miyuki, a radical feminist, as she has an affair with a woman; conceives a child with an African-American soldier stationed in Okinawa (in a phone conversation, her mother suggests that she kill the baby); starts a day care centre for prostitutes; distributes pamphlets to prostitutes (which, an intertitle states, leads to Hara's being beaten by gangsters); joins a feminist commune; and works as a stripper in a GI bar, all the while arguing with Hara and his lover, Kobayashi, also the sound-recordist and producer of the film. Like Imamura's *Buta to gunkan* (*Pigs and Battleships*, 1961), Hara's film paints a savage portrait of a Japanese port town corrupted by the American naval presence. Hara explained his reasons for making this confessional work:

> In the sixties and seventies, there was a feeling that if the individual did not cause change, nothing would change. At the time, I wanted to make a movie, and I was wondering how I could make a statement for change. At the time, there was much talk of family-imperialism [*kazoku teikokushugi*]. One of the strong sentiments of the time was that family-imperialism should be destroyed. I thought that if I could put my own family

under the camera, all our emotions, our privacy, I wondered if I might break taboos about the family.[11]

In *Extreme Private Eros: Love Song 1974*, Hara sought to explore ties between the "family-system" (*kazoku seido*) and the "emperor-system" (*tennōsei*). The darkly autobiographical documentary startled audiences in Japan, and became the talk of the film community. Hara's inclusion of seemingly self-humiliating scenes – at one point, Takeda warns Kobayashi: "He's only after your body; he's certainly not good in bed" – led the critic Saitō Masaharu to conclude that Hara had made the transition from sadism to masochism. Hara dismisses these labels:

> When the subject of my film was perceived to be stronger than I, as Takeda Miyuki was, I was called a masochist; when the subject was perceived to be weaker, I was called a sadist. Instead of being a masochist or a sadist, I would say that the nature of documentary filmmaking is that the director puts himself in various situations.[12]

Like many avant-garde works, *Extreme Private Eros: Love Song 1974* ignores established conventions of cinematic style. The sound is never synchronous with the grainy black and white scenes; in many instances, there is a radical disjunction between the location-recorded sound and the images. Like Jonas Mekas' *Reminiscences of a Journey to Lithuania* (1972), Hara's film has a strong home-movie flavour accentuated by jump cuts, flash-frames, few establishing shots, first-person voice-over and a handheld camera, although Hara uses relatively long takes as opposed to Mekas' fragmentation of time and space. Hara's voice-over has the same halting, emotional tone as Mekas' narration, and the non-synchronous sound accentuates the feeling of dislocation and loss.[13]

Hara states in the voice-over that "the only way to keep the relationship was to make a film". Here, as in Ross McElwee's *Sherman's March* (1985), the camera offers a bridge to intimate contact with others, a pretext for interaction. The filmmaker does not passively record reality, but rather provokes certain encounters. Of his methods, Hara later noted: "I am not the type of director to shoot something just happening [like a demonstration], but rather I like to make something happen and then shoot it".[14] His documentaries are virtual collaborations – along the lines of the ethnographic fictions of Jean Rouch such as *Moi, un noir* (*Me, a Black*, 1957)[15] – in which the director encourages the subjects to perform their lives for the camera. In Hara's words: "Life is acting. There are two sides to people. The person one wants to be, and the person one is. I want the people in my movies to act the way they want to be."[16]

After the scandal of *Extreme Private Eros: Love Song 1974*, thirteen years passed before Hara released another feature. During this time, he supported himself by freelance work on fiction films. He worked as an assistant cameraman on Imamura's *Fukūshu suru wa ware ni ari* (*Vengeance is Mine*, 1979) and *Eijanaika* (1981), and as an assistant director on Urayama Kirio's *Taiyō no ko* (*The Children of the Sun*, 1980) and Kumai Kei's *Umi to dokuyaku* (*Sea and Poison*, 1986). The unanticipated success of *The Emperor's Naked Army Marches On* dramatically changed Hara's life. It made him a major figure in film in Japan and on the international art-house circuit. He travelled abroad for the first time, attending festivals where his feature won numerous awards. Later, he obtained a year-long fellowship to visit the United States, where he studied at New York University with Christine Choy (co-director of *Who Killed Vincent Chin?* [1987]) and also spent countless hours viewing films at the Museum of Modern Art.

The profits from *The Emperor's Naked Army Marches On* facilitated the production of Hara's most recent film, *Zenshin shōsetsuka* (*A Dedicated Life*, 1994), about the short story writer, Inoue Mitsuharu. All of Hara's unorthodox "action documentaries" have implicitly raised questions about the boundary between fiction and non-fiction. With *A Dedicated Life*, Hara sought to focus directly on this issue by tracing how Inoue weaves fiction from everyday experiences. Hara initially planned to film the writer for ten years. The production took an unexpected turn, however. Shortly after shooting began in 1989, Inoue was diagnosed with cancer. The feature documentary traces his battle and eventual death from cancer while unravelling the fiction and reality of the writer's personal mythology. Inoue, it becomes clear, was an inveterate liar.

During a clip from a television appearance, Inoue, burning with resentment, tells how his father missed the application deadline for élite junior secondary schools. Inoue insists that, with his high grades, he would have easily won entrance. His younger sister, however, recalls that Inoue failed the exam. The repeated revelations of the writer's invented past provide much of the humour of *A Dedicated Life*. Inoue claims that his first love was a Korean girl who dropped out of his junior secondary school to join a brothel. Inoue supposedly went to see her there one evening, only to end up having his first sexual experience with a much older prostitute. Asked about this brothel, one surprised elementary school acquaintance, who never left the town in question, has no memory of such a place. Another classmate confirms the fiction of Inoue's adolescent escapade. To accentuate its fabricated nature, Hara stages a fictional sequence, using actors, of Inoue's tale of first love. In all likelihood, the director will continue to explore the line between fiction and documentary. Hara has spent the past few years developing a feature film based on the life of an infamous Japanese murderess. His most recent documentary, *Urayama Kirio no shozo* (*The Life of Urayama Kirio*, 1998), is a portrait of the film director Urayama Kirio, who began as an assistant to Imamura at Nikkatsu Studios. Hara is currently a visiting professor at Waseda University.

In the name of the Emperor: the historical context

In February 1972, the Japanese soldier Yokoi Shōichi returned home from the jungle of Guam, where he had continued to fight the Pacific War, unaware that Japan had surrendered 27 years earlier. Upon arriving at Haneda Airport in Tokyo, Yokoi stated: "Embarrassing as it is, I have returned alive. I brought back the rifle that I received from the Emperor."[17] Yokoi remained loyal to the Emperor in whose name the war was fought. In 1975, Yokoi was surprised to hear the Shōwa Emperor (Hirohito) publicly blame the war on the militarists:

> The Emperor really said something unexpected. I believed from the bottom of my heart that I went to war as a child of the Emperor according to the Emperor's orders. Now the Emperor says, 'The war was started by the militarists who used me. I could not say "No".'...Honestly, I am disappointed.[18]

Yokoi's disappointment in the Shōwa Emperor was shared by many veterans who were told after Japan's surrender that he was a pacifist who never supported the war. Some have refused to countenance this abrupt about-face. Okuzaki Kenzō, the protagonist of *The Emperor's*

Naked Army Marches On, holds the Emperor personally responsible for the disastrous conflict.

The Japanese interviewed in Haruko Taya Cook and Theodore F Cook's *Japan at War: An Oral History* (1992) often refer to the Emperor as the reason they supported the war. Ogawa Tamotsu says: "I really believed it my duty to serve as a Japanese soldier – one of His Majesty's Children".[19] Miyagi Kikuko tries to explain how she could have taken part in a war deemed stupid by younger people: "For us the Emperor and the Nation were supreme. For them, one should not withhold one's life".[20] Naval officer Kojima Kiyofumi remembers facing starvation in the jungle in the Philippines, and leading a group of soldiers to surrender:

> As we came down from the mountains and approached the enemy, the two army men urged the rest of us to go on ahead because they had such terrible diarrhea. I suggested that we all rest instead. Later, they repeated their request. Finally they said they didn't want to surrender. As two members of the Imperial Army, they'd rather 'die for the sake of the Emperor.' They asked me to leave them a hand grenade as we left them.[21]

Japanese soldiers were forbidden by Imperial Rescript from surrendering, and those few who did often brought shame on their families.

The Emperor's Naked Army Marches On explores Japanese memories of the Pacific War, forcing repressed events into consciousness. What has the war meant to the Japanese people? While Americans remember the Second World War as "the good war",[22] Japanese remember it as a bad war. There was a time, however, when the conflict was going well for Japan. Japan's war began in 1931 with its invasion and eventual annexation of Manchuria. Hostilities with China escalated into full-scale war in July 1937. The Japanese military's tactics were often vicious, with widespread indiscriminate killing of civilians, use of poisonous gas, and even use of prisoners of war for gruesome medical experiments. Japan's war against the Allies began with the attack on Pearl Harbor in December 1941. After a series of lightning victories, Japan, by mid-1942, controlled one seventh of the world's land. At that time, the closest adviser to the Shōwa Emperor recorded in his diary that the Emperor's "face was especially radiant, and he was smiling".[23]

From mid-1942, however, Japan suffered defeat after defeat. By autumn 1944, it was clear to many Japanese leaders that their country had no hope of victory; the fighting nevertheless continued for another year. During this final period, casualties increased dramatically; Japanese soldiers died by the hundreds of thousands throughout the Pacific. Okuzaki Kenzō was near death when he was captured in New Guinea in 1944; he was nursed back to health in an American field hospital.[24] He thus missed the most brutal phase of the New Guinea campaign. Only 30 of the more than 1000 members of Okuzaki's unit, the 36th Engineering Corps, survived. Including Okuzaki, ten of these survivors appear in *The Emperor's Naked Army Marches On*. Approximately 148 000 Japanese soldiers died in New Guinea during the war.[25]

Japan surrendered unconditionally on 15 August 1945. Japanese casualties, including civilians, numbered nearly three million, while Japanese occupation caused the deaths of millions more throughout areas in Asia.[26] With the end of the war, the Japanese began the process of mourning, remembering, and distributing blame for the "bad war". The Far East International Military Tribunal, staged by the Allies and dominated by American authorities, provided one interpretation of war guilt; seven war criminals – "militarists" – were executed in 1948.

The Shōwa Emperor played a critical role in ending the conflict in August 1945, after the atomic bombings of Hiroshima and Nagasaki, and the Soviet Union's entry into the Pacific War. Glorification of this decision, however, has served to mute questions about his responsibility for a war that lasted fifteen of the first twenty years of his reign. The glorification began with Prime Minister Suzuki Kantarō's speech to the nation on the day Japan surrendered: "His Majesty made the sacred decision to end the war in order to save the people...the nation sincerely apologizes to His Majesty [for the way the war ended]".[27] A few weeks later, Suzuki's successor, Prince Naruhiko Higashikuni, reiterated the message in his opening speech to the Diet:

> The termination of the war has been brought about solely through the benevolence of our Sovereign. It was His Majesty himself, who, apologizing to the spirits of the Ancestors, decided to save the millions of His subjects from privation and misery, and to pave the way for an era of grand peace for generations to come.[28]

Politicians immediately provided interpretations of the Emperor's heroic role and blamed the defeat on the people. Later, responsibility would be shifted to the militarists.

The Japanese government and, for their own political reasons, the American authorities who ran the Occupation distanced the Emperor from the war. In November 1945, the Cabinet headed by Prime Minister Shidehara Kijūrō issued a report which stressed that the Shōwa Emperor bore no war responsibility.[29] American authorities exempted the Emperor from trial as a war criminal, but stripped him of sovereignty, rewriting the constitution to make him "the symbol of the State and of the unity of the people". New clothes were tailored for the Emperor to change his image. The Imperial Household Agency choreographed nationwide tours by the Shōwa Emperor. Covering nearly the entire country between 1946 and 1954, the Emperor, his generalissimo outfit replaced with suit and tie, walked among the people to encourage them to rebuild Japan into a peaceful nation.[30] Debated for a brief period during the early years of the occupation, the issue of the Emperor's war responsibility gradually became taboo.

This remaking of the figure of the Emperor, symbol of Japan, contributed to the reconstruction of Japanese national identity. Soothing myths transformed the image of the country from aggressor to victim. The Shōwa Emperor's character and historical role, in its orthodox form, came to be depicted as follows. Firstly, he was a long-time pacifist, as symbolised by his courageous decision to end the war. Secondly, although he disagreed with the decisions of his ministers during the pre-war and wartime period, he acted as a constitutional monarch, simply sanctioning decisions made by others; in this way, he was rendered exempt from responsibility for the conflict.[31] The Emperor – like the Japanese people – was thus "victimised" by a tiny group of militarists hell-bent on war. With the subsequent purge of the extremists, the true pacifist nature of the Emperor and the Japanese nation blossomed. Popular postwar films such as Ōya Sōichi's *Nihon no ichiban nagai hi* (*Japan's Longest Day*, 1967) propagated this myth of the Shōwa Emperor's historical role.[32]

In 1952, just before Japan regained independence, a young Dietman, Nakasone Yasuhiro, raised the question of the Emperor's moral responsibility for the war in the House of Representatives. Nakasone proceeded carefully in his interpellation of Prime Minister Yoshida Shigeru. After making an obligatory reference to the

Emperor's pacifist nature, Nakasone asked the government's opinion on a possible abdication in order to renew the monarchy and console the victims of the war. An enraged Yoshida responded that anyone who proposed the abdication of the beloved Emperor was a non-citizen or un-Japanese (*hikokumin*).[33]

This exchange between Yoshida and Nakasone became well-known only after Nakasone became Prime Minister 30 years later. By the early 1980s, Nakasone upheld the official line. While he was Prime Minister, Nakasone, like Yoshida before him, defended the Shōwa Emperor as a pacifist who bore no war responsibility.[34] Furthermore, by trumpeting distinctive symbols such as the Imperial House and the Japanese flag, Nakasone worked to reinforce the feeling of national community among the Japanese. He was the first to make a highly symbolic "official visit as Prime Minister" to Yasukuni Shrine on the anniversary of the surrender. Until the occupation authorities ended state support, this site was the official monument to Japanese war dead. Re-establishing state support has long been a goal of conservative politicians, and Yasukuni Shrine remains a symbol for those who still look favourably upon Japan's wartime actions.

Appropriately, Nakasone's period as Prime Minister (1982-87), overlaps exactly the years during which *The Emperor's Naked Army Marches On* was in production. Born in 1918, Nakasone comes from the same generation as Okuzaki. Both men served in the military during the Pacific War – Nakasone as a naval officer and Okuzaki as a private in the Army. In 1946, Okuzaki returned to Japan from a prisoner-of-war camp in Australia only to find his mother emaciated and blind from lack of food. Distraught at not being able to provide for her family, she had nearly succeeded in hanging herself shortly before his return.[35] Both veterans came to question the Emperor's war responsibility. Early in his political career, Nakasone was dismissed as a non-citizen by the Prime Minister for voicing these concerns in the Diet. Okuzaki, for his part, delights in calling himself un-Japanese, using the term *hikokumin* to describe himself in the title of one of his recent books.[36] He has pursued his inquest into the Emperor's historical role in a direct manner, using a slingshot to fire *pachinko* balls at the Emperor. Okuzaki explained the reasons for his 1969 attack: "As a soldier during the war I suffered. All my combat buddies died, and I hate the person most responsible for the war, the Emperor."[37]

The making of *The Emperor's Naked Army Marches On*

In the late-1970s, Okuzaki Kenzō asked Imamura Shōhei to direct a film about his life. Imamura had, by that time, made a series of remarkable films about the Pacific War for Japanese Television, including *Muhō Matsu kokyō ni kaeru* (*Matsuo the Untamed Comes Home*, 1974), about a veteran who returns to Nagasaki for the first time after 33 years abroad. Although fascinated by Okuzaki's story, Imamura eventually abandoned the venture when he recognised that it was too controversial to be broadcast on television. The director suggested the project to Hara, who had worked on Imamura's *Vengeance is Mine* and *Eijanaika* as an assistant cameraman. Imamura arranged for Hara and Okuzaki to meet in February 1981. (For his substantial contribution, Imamura receives the first credit, "Planning by", on *The Emperor's Naked Army Marches On*.) By early 1982, although Okuzaki remained sceptical of Hara's abilities, they had agreed to make a film together.

Hara and his wife, Kobayashi Sachiko, produced the documentary independently through their company, Shissō Productions, without funds from Japanese Television or any of the major film studios. "[N]o companies would give me money", Hara recalled, "so I borrowed money from friends. It was really a film that could only be made independently. I had no money, but I had time and freedom. Time and freedom were weapons to make a film about a taboo subject."[38] Imamura assisted with the financing, and Okuzaki himself provided some of the funds. Throughout 1982 and 1983, Hara shot some 40 hours of 16mm film, using a small crew. Over a difficult five-year period, Hara produced, directed, shot and edited the film. The two-hour documentary eventually cost about 30 000 000 yen (or $250 000 at 120 yen to the dollar).

Hara conceived of this work as a means of confronting the historical legacy of the Pacific War. He noted:

> Military 'organizations' continue to exist today in Japan. The Nanking Massacre, the experiments conducted on humans by Unit 731, etc., even among the victims, there are few people willing to talk about such events. Why? The war is over, so why don't they talk about it? Because the war values continue to exist in Japanese

society. I wanted to film the segment of Japanese society that still maintains values of the wartime era.[39]

Before the shooting began, Hara met with ex-Sergeant Yamada Kichitarō, who provided the list of members of the 36th Engineering Corps. This list was used to track down the veterans of the New Guinea campaign. The ex-Sergeant had more fully readjusted to postwar life than had his old friend, Okuzaki; Yamada raised a family and even sent his children to college. Hara planned to film Yamada's story concurrently with that of Okuzaki, but the veteran fell ill and was hospitalised.

At this point, the subject-matter of the film was still broadly defined as a portrait of the war generation. Okuzaki's political activities embraced many different aspects of the fifteen-year conflict, including the Nanking Massacre.[40] Hara has described his exploratory approach to non-fiction: "This is a real difference between documentaries and drama films. The director himself doesn't understand what will happen. This was certainly the case with *The Emperor's Naked Army Marches On*. I had no idea how that film would turn out when I was making it."[41] Through his own research, the director obtained conclusive evidence of the illegal executions of several Army privates. Only after the filming of ex-Sergeant Takami Minoru did Hara narrow his focus to the murder of Japanese soldiers by their superior officers during the New Guinea campaign.

Throughout the production, Hara discussed possible scenes with his protagonist. The director filmed Okuzaki visiting the graves of his mother and of his father's ancestors, scenes which do not appear in the finished work. Okuzaki routinely phoned Hara at six o'clock in the morning with ideas for the documentary, including, for example, a wedding ceremony in which the elderly veteran would act as a traditional go-between, and a trip to western New Guinea to erect memorials for dead Japanese soldiers. Okuzaki was as overbearing a star as any filmmaker could ever find. The director recalled that his outlandish subject was always fighting with the crew: "Some of the younger staff members quit. I, too, really came to dislike Okuzaki. He was chaotic. In the film he sounds logical only because of skillful editing. The way he speaks is often incoherent."[42] At numerous points during the shooting, the erratic veteran withdrew from the project. In one case, he threatened to burn all of the accumulated footage in Tokyo.

In another instance, Okuzaki berated Hara for shooting an encounter in which he receives a beating from an irate ex-Sergeant; he felt it inappropriate for the hero of the film to be shown during a moment of weakness. The veteran even spoke of kidnapping the 77-year-old Shimamoto Iseko, against her family's wishes, to take her to the village in New Guinea where her son was buried. Okuzaki's involvement in the making of the documentary was so substantial that he considers himself to be the director as well as the star. From his prison cell, he even wrote and published his own review of *The Emperor's Naked Army Marches On*.[43] When Hara visited him at Hiroshima Prison in 1987, the indefatigable activist said: "Without fail I will leave this place healthy. I would by all means like you to film the scene when I leave."[44]

Shortly after the filmed encounter with ex-medic Hamaguchi Masaichi, Okuzaki disclosed his intention to murder one of his former officers, hoping to convince the director to record the homicide. "I want to kill Koshimizu and I would like you to film it", the veteran told Hara. "No movie has such a scene in it. Having you film such a scene would be my greatest present to you."[45] Hara discussed the issue at length with his lawyer, his producer and other directors. The filmmaker recalled:

> This was a very delicate problem. I had to decide if I should film it or not. I still have not made up my mind. One reason that I didn't film it is that I had become really sick of Okuzaki. I might have filmed it. Human beings have dark sides, and people want to see something frightening. People want to see the evil side of people. A little bit of me says I would like to see it. I went to speak to Imamura. His opinion was really different. He told me not to do it.[46]

When Hara mentioned his misgivings, Okuzaki told him: "You're no good".[47] Later, during a five-hour conversation in Kobe, producer Kobayashi implored Okuzaki not to kill anyone.

In March 1983, Okuzaki returned for two weeks to western New Guinea (now known as Irian Jaya) with Hara and assistant director, Yasuoka Takuji. Under the best of circumstances, filming of this pivotal sequence would be difficult. Ever since the transfer of the territory from The Netherlands to Indonesia in 1963, a low-level guerrilla war for independence had been fought there. In 1983, access to many areas was restricted by Indonesian authorities. At Okuzaki's request, Hara and Yasuoka reluctantly agreed to pose as the nephews of Private Shimamoto Masayuki to facilitate a visit to his burial ground in Arso. During the delicate negotiations to obtain permission to travel to the interior, Okuzaki became increasingly abrasive, berating officials and crew. Much to Hara's amazement, authorisation was granted to visit the village. In Arso and other towns such as Abepura, Okuzaki commemorated fallen Japanese comrades. Hara also filmed the veteran's return to Demta, the village where he was taken prisoner in 1944.

On the last day of the exhausting trip, at Okuzaki's request, Hara filmed him thanking the police for their cooperation. When an alarmed officer requested the footage in the camera, Okuzaki insulted him. In response, the policeman demanded all of their film. The director was obliged to surrender 50 rolls of 16mm stock to Indonesian authorities, some two hours and fourteen minutes, all of the footage shot in the territory. Hara was distraught. The crew returned to Tokyo empty-handed. At Narita Airport, Okuzaki spat on his passport before handing it over to Japanese customs officials, and then later berated Hara for his failure to refer to him as *Sensei* (master). Okuzaki's intransigence only further damaged their attempts to obtain the confiscated footage. In spite of concerted efforts through diplomatic and private channels, Hara and his producer were never able to retrieve the exposed film.

Shortly after their dispiriting return to Japan, Okuzaki tried to convince the director to accompany him to the eastern half of the island, now Papua New Guinea, to visit the Wewak Garrison where the 36th Engineering Corps had been stationed. The veteran intended to retrace his retreat through the jungle and illegally cross the frontier between Papua New Guinea and Irian Jaya. Hara refused and thereafter had virtually no contact with Okuzaki. Some eight months later, in December 1983, he learned from a television news report that the veteran was a suspect in a shooting. Although Okuzaki was quickly apprehended, later newscasts detailed a substantially larger plot of political assassinations. Okuzaki had targeted several politicians of the Jiyū Minshutō (Liberal Democratic Party), some employees of the Indonesian Consulate in Kobe, and one Japanese veteran involved in the Nanking Massacre.

Dismayed, Hara put aside the unedited footage for two years, convinced that without the confiscated New Guinea sequences he had no film. Only in 1986 did the director attempt to edit the rushes, by and large following the chronology of the shoot. The most difficult task was to bring some coherence to Okuzaki's rambling declarations, and to outline the confusing events of the New Guinea campaign, especially those leading up to the execution incidents. Where necessary, the director added intertitles to explain the unfolding investigation. He avoided archival footage because of its conventional associations. At private previews, the unrestrained laughter of young audience-members astounded Hara. Much to his surprise, the completed documentary received the 1986 New Director's Prize from the Directors' Guild of Japan, a vote of confidence from the film community for a highly unorthodox work.

After initial festival screenings, Hara applied for a grant from the Kawakita Memorial Film Institute to make 35mm prints for theatrical release in Japan and abroad. At this time, the documentary received its controversial English-language title, *The Emperor's Naked Army Marches On*. (*Yukiyukite shingun* literally translates as "Forward, Divine Army".) The director recalled that a gentleman at the institute volunteered to think of a title in English, a gracious offer he could not easily refuse:

> It's a little embarrassing. The sense is different in English than in the original Japanese. At the time, however, I didn't understand that – I had not yet been abroad, you know. The character '*shin*' is very difficult to translate; one might say God but that is not the exact sense in Japanese. The English title suggests that Okuzaki continues to fight for the emperor. At the time, it seemed like a title that foreign audiences could understand. This is what the man who attached the English title insisted. At the time, I agreed. The title is ironic, but it turned out well.[48]

While some Japanese critics, such as Karatani Kōjin, find the English title terribly misleading, it does convey a sense of Okuzaki's fanaticism. Furthermore, this problem was not limited to the English-speaking world. *Cahiers du Cinéma*, for example, cites the French title as *L'armée de l'empereur s'avance* ("The Emperor's Army Marches On"), an even more deceptive translation.[49]

Character analysis: Okuzaki as action hero

Although embodying some of the traits of an action star in *The Emperor's Naked Army Marches On*, Okuzaki Kenzō cuts an unusual figure as a hero, much less as a movie star. At 62 years of age (as an intertitle informs us), slight of build, with a mouthful of crooked teeth, sporting, at the outset, a red "Yuasa Battery" automotive jacket, the veteran of the New Guinea campaign strikes a rather pitiful appearance. Yet, he is tireless and fearless. This type fits Hara's preference for strong, decisive characters, such as Batman and Superman: "I love Hollywood action films, and I wanted Okuzaki to act like an action star".[50] Never distracted by romance, monetary considerations or the demands of daily living, Okuzaki pursues his political agenda single-mindedly. His worldly concerns are few; viewers scarcely learn of his day job as a car mechanic.

Okuzaki's commitment to social activism is total. Painted political slogans adorn the façade of his store, as well as the sides of his mobile sound-truck. One reads "All men are equal – there are no authority figures such as the Emperor". Although opponents and allies emerge over the course of the film, the veteran never pauses to re-evaluate his methods, nor does he ever express doubt. On the contrary, he spends every free moment erecting monuments for dead soldiers, praying for their souls, badgering living veterans, and staging direct protests against the Japanese government. When the sister and brother of two murdered soldiers abandon the investigation, Okuzaki continues without them. Not to be undone by their refusal to accompany him on further interviews, he nonchalantly substitutes others in their roles as grieving relatives.

Although cast in the mould of a hero, Okuzaki is not a larger-than-life figure. Rather, he represents the ordinary, even anonymous, Japanese man of his generation. Born in 1920 to a poor family, he came of age during the 1930s, a period of rising militarism as Japan sought to expand its empire. Like millions of his compatriots, he was conscripted into the military upon reaching adulthood and took part in a war fought in the name of the Emperor. Unlike his fellow countrymen, however, he has insisted upon lifting the veil of silence that has obscured the painful war years. In Nagata, Kobe, where he has tracked down Hamaguchi Masaichi, at a restaurant, he accosts the owners: "All you want is money! These people lost their brothers. Which is more important? Forget about money!" Unimpressed by his country's postwar commercial boom, Okuzaki has abandoned his former anonymity for a unique position in Japanese culture as a proponent of violent civil disobedience.

Okuzaki, like Prime Minister Nakasone, has a keen grasp of political symbolism; rather than support official symbols, however, he attacks them. On 29 April 1982, during the Shōwa Emperor's birthday, a national holiday, the veteran stages a protest "to console the souls of the many victims who died for the Emperor during the Pacific War". His sound-truck, from which he blares anti-Emperor announcements, sports two flags which parody the Japanese flag. Whereas the official flag has a white background and a red centre (the rising sun), the veteran's version inverts this colour scheme. Over the loudspeaker, he shouts: "Okuzaki Kenzō is here, on Emperor's Day. The Emperor is 81 years old and still on the throne. Many soldiers died for him and his group." Before he is carted away by the police, Okuzaki takes the opportunity to criticise the entire political Establishment, including the Nihon Kyōsantō (Japan Communist Party), for opportunism.

Through additional symbolic gestures, the veteran acknowledges the political import of war memorials. In several scenes, he raises grave markers for dead comrades (as he did in Irian Jaya in the confiscated footage). At the end of the documentary, Okuzaki attacks another veteran for insisting that he has paid his respects to the executed soldiers by visiting Yasukuni Shrine, considered by conservatives to be the proper memorial to the war dead. "You think that by your going to Yasukuni Shrine the spirits of the dead are consoled?", an agitated Okuzaki yells while moving in to strike the ex-Sergeant. As the activist recognises, this shrine remains part of the ideological structure that encouraged Japanese unquestioningly to support the war in the first place.

Okuzaki's activities, especially his anti-Emperor protests, have estranged him from mainstream Japanese society. Nevertheless, he perseveres. In *The Emperor's Naked Army Marches On*, he obstinately implicates the Shōwa Emperor whenever possible, denouncing him as "the most cowardly man in Japan" and "a symbol of ignorance and irresponsibility". With only minor support from others, he is virtually a one-man social movement. As noted in an intertitle at the beginning of the film, only incompletely translated in the English subtitles, Okuzaki's convictions include: "1956: Murder of a real estate broker, ten years at hard labour. 1969: Shooting of a sling at the Emperor in the palace, one year and six months. 1976: Scattering pornographic handbills of the Emperor, one year and two months.

1981: Plotting to murder ex-Prime Minister Tanaka Kakuei, not indicted." Proud of his convictions, Okuzaki sees himself as a warrior in a crusade. Above all, he is a man of action, as Hara noted: "Okuzaki threw *pachinko* balls at the emperor. But intellectuals, you know, they debate ideas, but they can't *do* anything."[51]

With boundless energy, Okuzaki dominates the screen. Of the 30 scenes which comprise *The Emperor's Naked Army Marches On*, he appears fully in 24. (Three of the remaining six consist primarily of printed intertitles.) Even his interactions with his wife, Shizumi, are determined by political expediency. At the beginning of scene 5, she dutifully presents him with a packed lunch and a wrapped gift for his day of protest. Later, during confrontations with accused veterans in scenes 21-23, Mrs Okuzaki impersonates, at her husband's request, the relatives of various soldiers killed in New Guinea. In scene 25, she even throws herself between her enraged husband and ex-Sergeant Yamada, taking a blow to her leg that was intended for the elderly veteran. Standing in front of a Red Cross hospital, Okuzaki thanks her for her sacrifice: "She did well. I appreciate it. She saved me." Mrs Okuzaki serves as an accomplice and sidekick to the eccentric hero. Later, after her husband's imprisonment for attempted murder, Shizumi picks up where he left off, announcing his intentions over the loudspeaker of their mobile van.

While fearless and willing to take responsibility for his acts, Okuzaki behaves erratically, attacking his interviewees at one point, excusing himself the next. Time after time, he is belligerent, stubborn and self-aggrandising. He takes every opportunity to point out to his fellow veterans that the postwar life he has lived is superior to theirs. Okuzaki shows cunning, but little wit, in his pursuit of the accused veterans. Since he takes himself completely seriously, his speeches and actions, while often humorous, are only inadvertently so. When Okuzaki assigns his wife the role of grieving relative, he finally cracks a slight smile and laughs at himself; otherwise, he seems totally unself-conscious.

On occasion, Okuzaki also acts politely and solicitously. Speaking on the phone with the Chief of Surveillance for the Hyogo Police, he engages in a formal, ritualised exchange of pleasantries. (At the same time, he makes sure to record their conversation with a wiretap.) During most of his confrontations, the veteran continues to use the appropriate hierarchical forms of address demanded by the Japanese language. Despite the utter unconventionality of his surprise visits, he always comes bearing presents, as custom requires. Dropping in on Takami Minoru in Yagake, Okayama, Okuzaki apologises for the insufficiency of his gift: "I should have brought something better". When the veterans confess their crimes, Okuzaki becomes forgiving and understanding. He expresses concern over ex-Sergeant Yamada's difficulty with urination just moments after he has attacked the elderly veteran with blows from hands and feet.

Occasionally, Okuzaki presents a gentle bearing, especially during the mourning scenes, when he becomes uncharacteristically modest. His grief, which he shares with the family members of the infantrymen, is not that of a political opportunist. In Etajima, Hiroshima, he introduces himself to Shimamoto Iseko, whose son he buried with his own hands in Arso, New Guinea. Bowing and sobbing, Okuzaki says: "Unfortunately he died, but he was lucky to have been buried. I think he was happy. So I want to console his soul my way." His feelings for the soldiers, privates killed during the prime of their youth, appear utterly genuine.

Okuzaki explicitly rejects the hierarchies of the family, the military and the nation. He retains a healthy notion of individual responsibility as regards the Emperor and the soldiers who committed crimes during the war. The veteran Takami reiterates an explanation made notorious by Nazi officials at the Nuremburg Trials, "An order is an order, we had to obey", a rationalisation which Okuzaki rejects. When ex-Sergeant Seo claims that "In the Army orders always came first", Okuzaki beats him to the ground. The protagonist brushes aside the veterans' appeals to military hierarchy, while at the same time recognising that superior officers bear special responsibilities for actions taken in their names: "I'm accusing the Emperor for the same reason. He was responsible as the Supreme Commander of the Imperial Army."

Okuzaki maintains that his social movement is divinely inspired. He visits Yamada Kichitarō at a hospital in Fukaya, and tells him that his illness represents "divine punishment" for his wartime activities. During his protest of Emperor's Day at a Tokyo intersection, Okuzaki proclaims his iconoclastic version of heroism over the loudspeaker of his mobile van: "A great man observes God's law, not man's law, without fearing man's punishment". Later, he recounts how he spat on the judge presiding over one of his trials, demonstrating his contempt for the law. Like the vigilantes of American detective films, he works for justice through extralegal means, outside a system he defines as corrupt. The protagonist of a hard-boiled crime story is typically, as John G Cawelti notes, "a private investigator who occupies a marginal position with respect to the official social institutions of criminal justice".[52] Like the classic action hero, Okuzaki has to resort to violence to bring the guilty to justice. Incapable of compromise, Okuzaki's awkward nobility derives from the righteousness of his moral beliefs and the justness of his cause.

Although he claims divine inspiration, Okuzaki is a radical empiricist, steadfastly attached to a series of particular events that occurred in New Guinea at the end of the Pacific War. Unlike the relatives of the victims, he does not accept the *Rashomon*-like consequences of the conflicting testimonies obtained from the veterans.[53] Instead, Okuzaki pieces together the traces of the illegal executions by an obstinate attention to the exact details of how many bullets were fired, where the principals were standing, and the direction in which the bodies fell. Like the woman in Alain Resnais' *Hiroshima, mon amour* (1959), Okuzaki refuses to live in the present, to forget, and to get on with his life as so many of the other veterans have done. He remains resolutely, even courageously, stuck in the past.

Imploring ex-Sergeant Yamada to confess, Okuzaki calls on the survivor of the New Guinea occupation to acknowledge the terrible truths of war because "fact is fact". As in Kurosawa Akira's *Ikimono no kiroku* (*Record of a Living Being*, 1955), the main character's mad obsession with the war disturbs the surface calm of the present. The injustices of history are, for Okuzaki, fresh wounds that call for redress and revenge. Like a vengeful spirit, he comes back to avenge the slain soldiers. Although clearly no ghost, he embodies the return of the repressed memory of Japan's military adventures during the Pacific War. This seems quite literally the case when Okuzaki abruptly shows up at the house of ex-Sergeant Takami, his superior officer whom he has not seen in the intervening 37 years. Dazed, Takami covers his face with his hat and tries to slip away.

Although working through extralegal means, Okuzaki maintains mostly cordial relations with the police. In scene 3, the veteran discusses his travel plans with the Chief of Surveillance for the Hyogo Police, a meeting which clearly indicates that his movements are monitored by Japanese authorities. At times, it seems as if Okuzaki desires their presence because it gives his protests a proper audience; he needs to be caught and punished to make his gesture of revolt complete. The police officers, for their part, consistently provide comic relief in *The Emperor's Naked Army Marches On*. Unlike Okuzaki and the veterans, the police remain anonymous. Although officers appear in six separate scenes, few of them are identified by name. Indeed, Okuzaki refers to the uniformed guards outside Kobe Prison as "robots" for refusing him entrance. Occasionally, policemen cover their faces in reaction to the camera; in front of the prison, they request that Hara stop filming. Several times, the police show up at the end of a heated confrontation between Okuzaki and one of the veterans. In at least one instance, Okuzaki himself calls them. In this absurd and comical twist, the perpetrator of the offence, not the victim, has requested their presence. Born after the Pacific War, the young officers are hardly equipped to address the controversial subject-matter. Understanding little of the situation, they are badgered by the unstable veteran and come across as faceless representatives of the social order.

Although frequently amusing, Okuzaki also appears dangerously unpredictable in his actions, capable of anything at times: aggression, violence, assassination. The roll-call of his prison sentences proves that he will go to any end to accomplish his goals. He is, after all, a convicted murderer. Throughout *The Emperor's Naked Army Marches On*, the viewer questions Okuzaki's sanity, although the filmmaker withholds judgment. Hara allows the veteran to state his case with conviction, even if he is insane. After Okuzaki has wrestled ex-Sergeant Seo Yukio to the ground, he implores him to speak openly of the past. When Seo responds that he has never met him before, Okuzaki yells, "I gave you my card", as if this social nicety justifies his violent actions. In his fanatical pursuit of the truth, Okuzaki represents a kind of comic anti-hero. Like most classic hero types, he remains a character without psychological depth, completely animated by duty to a higher goal. Hara never explores the roots of Okuzaki's erratic and grandiose behaviour in, for example, his family background. Nor does he offer an interpretation of Okuzaki's aggressive actions in terms of post-traumatic stress. Since Hara deliberately avoids all such forays into psychological motivations, viewers know almost nothing about Okuzaki at the end of the film.

Narrative analysis: anatomy of an investigation

Although *The Emperor's Naked Army Marches On* might be called an historical documentary, the film clings tenaciously to the present, rather than to the past. Hara explores the memory of the Pacific War, the resonance of the war years in the present, to "trace how the war survives in Japanese society today".[54] Similarly, while the film focuses on the activities of Okuzaki Kenzō, it skips over the details of his individual biography. Most historical documentaries – such as Connie Field's *The Life and Times of Rosie the Riveter* (1980), Noel Buckner/Mary Dore/Sam Sills' *The Good Fight* (1983) and Henry Hampton's *Eyes on the Prize* (1988) – use extensive archival footage, interviews with eyewitnesses and authoritative voice-over narration. Many also include interviews with scholars and journalists. Such conventional historical documentaries contribute to what Bill Nichols calls the "discourses of sobriety".[55]

Hara resists the didactic temptations of this form, instead focusing his story on the present-day activities of Okuzaki and the reactions that he provokes in others. Although the veteran frequently refers to the Emperor, Hara never cuts to footage or photographs of him. Nor is there any reference whatsoever to the atomic bomb, an unusual omission for a Japanese film about the Second World War, especially since Okuzaki visits Hiroshima repeatedly. Occasional photographs of soldiers appear, but they are usually found in the homes of the relatives whom the veteran visits. Hara focuses on the living memory of the war, like Claude Lanzmann, whose 9½-hour epic, *Shoah* (1985), chronicles the Holocaust in Europe without any archival imagery. Through synchronous sound interviews and images of the concentration camps as they appear 40 years after the war, Lanzmann anchors his film in the here-and-now to redeem the past and give the dead "an everlasting name".[56]

Hara's presence in *The Emperor's Naked Army Marches On* is more ambiguous than Lanzmann's moral stance in *Shoah*. The director never declares his thoughts about Okuzaki and the other veterans. Whereas the mass media treated Okuzaki as a lunatic whose actions were incomprehensible, Hara forces viewers to evaluate his character and activities without explicit editorial commentary. In addition, the director fails to intervene when Okuzaki assaults his interviewees. At these times, Hara holds back and observes the confrontations with apparent detachment, a voyeuristic posture that makes the viewer an inadvertent witness to violence. By putting the audience in the position of an accomplice, these scenes acutely pose questions about the ethics of documentary representation and the responsibilities of filmmakers towards their subjects.

Hara, unlike Lanzmann, does not conduct the interviews in his documentary. In *The Emperor's Naked Army Marches On*, he hovers in the background. The filmmaker's voice is only heard in the penultimate scene when he speaks to Mrs Okuzaki outside Hiroshima Prison. Nevertheless, there is no pretence that the camera is not there, as in the documentaries of Frederick Wiseman. On the contrary, throughout the two-hour film, the characters refer to the crew in passing, address the camera directly, and yell at the filmmakers. When Okuzaki presents Takami Minoru with a gift, the ex-Sergeant also bows in thanks to the off-camera film crew. At Hiroshima Prison, one of the guards places his hand over the camera lens. In the encounter with ex-Captain Koshimizu, Koshimizu's wife glides across the background and, directly facing the camera, takes a picture of the scene.

The Emperor's Naked Army Marches On deliberately restricts itself to its main character's world-view, plunging the viewer into a harrowing series of protests and confrontations with veterans and police. None of the other characters really gets the chance to call into question Okuzaki's methods and activities. (Through ironic juxtaposition and deliberate strokes of black comedy, the director manages to retain some independence from his protagonist.) Although Okuzaki confounds conventional divisions between left-wing and right-wing ideologies, he limits his political activities to crimes committed by Japanese officers against their fellow countrymen, and says little about the treatment of Chinese, Koreans or any other population colonised by Japan during the war. By confining the perspective of the film to the erratic veteran, however, the director directly confronts the audience with the moral chaos of the war.

The first third of *The Emperor's Naked Army Marches On* (scenes 1-10) introduces the principal character and his political activities. Although no story deadlines are immediately established, several possible narrative threads develop. The roll-call of prison sentences at the outset, given in chronological order, raises the spectre of future convictions. Having spent twelve years and eight months in jail, will Okuzaki go to prison again for his acts? In scene 3, he mentions plans to go to Tokyo. In scene 4, while visiting ex-Sergeant Yamada in the hospital, Okuzaki announces his intention to return to New Guinea. He hopes that Yamada will accompany him. During scene 8, he tries to convince Mrs Shimamoto, whose son died there, to come along as well. However, this narrative thread eventually peters out. Although Okuzaki later travelled to western New Guinea, an intertitle in scene 28 explains that the footage from the trip was confiscated there by Indonesian authorities. The veteran's return to the scene of the crime, therefore, turns out to be little more than a black hole in the story, a gap caused by the historical vagaries of colonialism and the Pacific War. Remarkably, director Hara calls attention to this missing sequence, highlighting the chance incompleteness of his narrative.

The introductory scenes alternate between tragedy and black comedy. The drama comes from the seriousness of the charges and the intensity of Okuzaki's involvement in the investigation. The dark humour emerges as he transgresses social norms in ways that are simultaneously disturbing and amusing. In the opening scene, a marriage ceremony, Okuzaki serves as a traditional intermediary between the bride and the groom. As a wedding song plays in the background, the viewer follows a procession of cars which bring the bride, the groom and the guests to the ceremony. Once everyone has arrived, commemorative photographs are taken. Now seated, the bride and groom sip sake from a cup held by others. Okuzaki's speech, entirely customary for a go-between, starts out innocently, maintaining the formality of the ritual, "I, Okuzaki Kenzō, am delighted to serve as go-between for the wedding of Miss Sano and Mr Otagaki. Congratulations on your wedding!" Without warning, however, the veteran then launches into an astonishing harangue:

> After graduating from Kobe University, the groom, Mr Otagaki, fought the Establishment. He was arrested. I, Okuzaki Kenzō, killed a real estate broker, shot *pachinko* balls at the Emperor, then scattered pornographic handbills of the Emperor in department stores. I served thirteen years in prison. My actions were all against the Establishment. This match was made because both the groom and the go-between fought the Establishment.

As Okuzaki concludes, "this is a rare wedding", the stunned viewer is inclined to agree.

Another traditional wedding tune is sung. Then, suddenly,

Okuzaki attacks the concept of nationhood: "Maybe this country [*kokka*] means a lot to you, but judging from my experience not only Japan but any other country is a wall between men. It stops them from joining each other. It's a big wall. I think a family is another wall. It isolates human beings from each other. It cuts ties. It's against divine law. So I attack it." Okuzaki implies that the nation is no more than an imagined community.[57] In case his listeners may be thinking of Japan as a family nation-state (headed by the Emperor), Okuzaki also lashes out at the institution of the family. Surely a wedding – an affirmation of tradition and the social order – is the last occasion where one would expect such a speech.

The veteran's tirade disturbs the content of the wedding, yet the couple still gets married. The ceremony ends outside with Okuzaki leading the participants in three shouts of "Congratulations!", as the newly-weds drive away. In the background, accentuating the absurdity of the sequence, Okuzaki's sound-truck holds a huge sign that reads, "Kill Tanaka Kakuei" [Prime Minister of Japan, 1972-74]. In addition, the director shoots the wedding scene from the level of the seated participants, using fixed framings in a parody of the studied camera style of Ozu Yasujirō.[58] Hara initially conceived of filming in a static, contemplative way, as a contrast to his earlier works, but his plans changed as he struggled to keep up with the energetic Okuzaki. As a result, the rest of the film has a ragged, handheld feel. Even for Japanese audiences, it travels at a frenetic pace, presenting a bewildering series of characters and arguments.

Okuzaki's outrageous yet funny actions continue. In scene 3, the eccentric veteran meets with the Chief of Surveillance for the Hyogo Police from whom he requests permission to go to Tokyo. Seeking to deter Okuzaki from staging a protest that will disrupt traffic (the very purpose of the trip), the officer suggests that he take the train. Okuzaki ignores the chief's suggestion and, in scene 5, stages a remarkable demonstration, only to be hauled away by the police. In scene 7, he argues with guards outside Kobe Prison, where he has come to take the measurements of a cell. Astonishingly, he wants to build a similar one in his own home in protest against the postwar political Establishment. Needless to say, the guards stonewall his attempt to enter the prison. In the face of Okuzaki's extremism, however, the officers' extraordinary restraint appears more ridiculous than commendable.

In the following scene, in a radical shift of tone, Okuzaki

shares with Shimamoto Iseko his grief over the death of her son. Sitting before his altar, with Okuzaki's encouragement, Mrs Shimamoto sings a halting, evocative song of mourning:

> Your mother has come to the pier,
> Again today, like any other day,
> Expecting your return from the war,
> Although I know you might be dead,
> Somewhere on the faraway battleground,
> If you're alive, if you're alive,
> You may be on the ship that carries,
> Repatriates to their homeland.

In the next two scenes, echoing traditional Japanese practices of ancestor worship, Okuzaki builds memorials in several Hyogo cemeteries for additional infantrymen who died during the war. The screen fills with the sounds of prayers and the soft crackle of fires built to prepare ritual offerings of food.

Scene 11 abruptly breaks this chorus of mourning, as Okuzaki once again moves to direct action, this time showing up unannounced at Takami Minoru's home in Okayama. The investigation of the execution of several Japanese soldiers in New Guinea, which will occupy the rest of *The Emperor's Naked Army Marches On*, begins here. "Weren't you there when Koshimizu shot the soldier named Yoshizawa?", Okuzaki bluntly asks the ex-Sergeant. A startled Takami – who, viewers later learn, lives under an assumed name – denies any first-hand knowledge of the events of 8 September 1945. During this encounter, Okuzaki identifies ex-Captain Koshimizu Masao, former leader of the Wewak Garrison, as the focus of his rage, announcing his intention to beat him. Bidding farewell to Takami, with an acute sense of the importance of his audience, the protagonist urges: "Keep watching me. I have many more things to do."

The investigation continues in earnest in scene 12. At this point, the film starts to take on some of the characteristics of a mystery or a courtroom drama. A series of charges, denials and countercharges are made by Okuzaki, the accused veterans, and relatives of the dead soldiers. Numerous witnesses are consulted as different hypotheses and motives are put forward to explain the deaths of Privates Yoshizawa and Nomura some three weeks after

Japan's surrender to the Allied powers. Okuzaki crisscrosses the Japanese mainland in search of his former comrades and their stories of the war. The director keeps the viewer aware of the national scope of the drama by detailing the locations in the intertitles: Tokyo, Hiroshima, Hyogo, Okayama, Yamanashi, Kobe and Shimane.

Okuzaki interrogates nine veterans of the Pacific War, either in person or on the telephone. Many of them have chosen lives of relative obscurity, and some have changed their names. Okuzaki shows up at their houses uninvited, in one instance yelling "Happy New Year!" as he enters. To one of the veterans he says, "Your wife seems to dislike making a film like this. I understand how she feels but does she know what it's all about?" The former member of the 36th Engineering Corps admits that his wife knows nothing of his experiences in New Guinea. Some of the characters maintain that the privates were executed for desertion, a violation punishable by death during wartime. Others suggest that desertion was a trumped-up charge used to get rid of troublesome soldiers. Even more harrowing motives are implied, such as cannibalism. Although the filmmaker periodically inserts intertitles to introduce, clarify and verify some aspects of the events described, the accusations emerge haphazardly over the course of the two-hour film, leaving the viewer in a state of perpetual anxiety over the disputed incidents and the identities of those involved. This frenzy of activity makes *The Emperor's Naked Army Marches On* a powerful and disconcerting documentary.

Okuzaki pursues his inquest like a zealous prosecutor. In scene 12, he ambushes Seo Yukio at his isolated homestead in Hakuta, Shimane. Standing outside the house, Okuzaki says: "I heard, Mr Seo, that you were at the spot where Private Yoshizawa was executed or, I'd rather say, murdered. Captain Koshimizu, the platoon leader, killed Private Yoshizawa with a gun." Seated on the floor, Seo, like Takami before him, denies any first-hand knowledge of the execution, maintaining that he was "away from the unit" when it occurred. Hoping to end the interview, Seo states: "I can't tell you all that happened. I'm busy today. I must go out." Okuzaki, insulted and suddenly enraged, attacks him and the two men wrestle to the ground, screaming at each other. Shown partly in slow-motion, the confrontation continues until Seo's wife and other family members arrive to restrain Okuzaki. This first outbreak of fighting will condition all the subsequent encounters between the old veterans. The perpetual threat of violence creates as much tension as does the search for the truth about the executions. (In scene 25, Okuzaki proudly states, "Violence is my forte".) As in several of the encounters, the interview with Seo ends with the arrival of the police, who cart Okuzaki away.

Scene 13 is one of the few in which the central protagonist does not appear. Sakimoto Rinko, the sister of Private Yoshizawa, provides independent verification of Okuzaki's contentions, maintaining that her brother was murdered. Her methods are also unorthodox: "I asked his soul at the altar yesterday to tell me how he died, exactly what happened. I chanted the sutra and prayed hard. Then his face moved. His face in the photo moved." In a subsequent confrontation, Sakimoto claims that her late brother "told" her of the circumstances surrounding his death. For the next four scenes, Sakimoto and Nomura Toshiya, the brother of executed Private Nomura Jinpei, accompany Okuzaki on his interviews. They take part in the encounters with the veterans Hara Toshio and Hamaguchi Masaichi, pivotal sequences that last twelve minutes each.

In scene 15, Okuzaki meets up with Sakimoto and Nomura outside a health centre in Iwasa, Yamanashi. Inside, in the lobby, they accost ex-Sergeant Hara. Following a brief exchange, they all retire to an office where Okuzaki pursues his inquiry into the executions of Yoshizawa and Nomura. The dramatic arc of this visceral scene oscillates between accusation and denial, until Hara Toshio makes a moving gesture of rapprochement towards the relatives. Then, the appearance of several policemen temporarily interrupts the rhythm of the interrogation. It returns once again when the officers leave and the scene concludes with a dramatic confession. Throughout the confrontation, the camera remains mostly at the level of the seated characters. The angles of the shots are cramped and numerous jump cuts occur. A harsh handheld light casts ungainly shadows on the walls, including that of the microphone boom. Both the camera and the accused veteran seem trapped in the small room.

Like Takami and Seo before him, Hara Toshio, at the outset of the interview, remains wilfully vague about his wartime experiences. The veteran blandly states: "My memories faded after many years". Both Nomura and Sakimoto aggressively question him, but to no avail. "The execution", an intertitle precisely notes, "took place twenty-three days after the war ended". Asked if he was a member of the firing squad, the ex-Sergeant says, "I don't know", to which Okuzaki replies incredulously, "You don't know? It's either 'yes' or 'no'". Leaning across the table, Sakimoto places a photograph of Yoshizawa in front of Hara Toshio, imploring him to tell the truth. Both relatives make appeals on behalf of the souls of the soldiers, as if the dead may only be laid to rest through public confessions.

After several minutes of equivocal responses, Okuzaki takes a more threatening stance, referring to his explosive encounter with Seo Yukio: "I didn't intend to beat him. But he refused to talk, so I hit him. Today, I came here planning to beat you. I can do it." Okuzaki's persistence and the presence of the grieving relatives, together with the framed photographs of their dead brothers, push the veteran towards a partial admission of guilt. Hara Toshio confirms the innocence of the two Army privates: "One thing I want to tell you. Your brothers, they did nothing wrong." Reaching across the long table, he clasps the hands of Nomura and then Sakimoto who refuses to let go. Sobbing, Sakimoto appeals to his generosity and goodwill. Wiping his eyes with a handkerchief, the ex-Sergeant states: "40 years after the war, the dead soldiers sleep in peace". Okuzaki and the relatives explicitly refute this. Sakimoto cries: "My brother appears in my dream. I see him in the altar, too. They aren't sleeping. They visit us."

The pressure increases on the veteran. Sakimoto refuses to leave until Hara Toshio tells the truth about the executions; she even threatens to follow him to his home. Okuzaki acknowledges his tactics: "It's a case of illegal confinement. But I don't care. I shot *pachinko* balls at the Emperor whom we'd worshipped. It was impossible for us soldiers to shoot at him. But I did. After I did this, my business increased 300% and people began to call me *Sensei*". Although often inarticulate, Okuzaki occasionally attains a level of eloquence in his arguments, as when he says to ex-Sergeant Hara, "Perhaps you want to return home but the two soldiers you shot, or shot at, can never return home from New Guinea".

As the atmosphere becomes more heated, several members of the Isawa Police suddenly arrive offscreen. Pounding on the table, Okuzaki invites them into the room, "Sit down here. You may arrest me. Come in. Who are you? You should learn more about life, about the war as a real story." Introducing himself, he bows deeply to the officers who, of course, respond in kind. When one policeman inadvertently blocks the view of the scene, Okuzaki instructs him to move out of the way of the crew: "I want the camera. We came here to shoot." Astonishingly, the two young officers slide over so as not to obstruct the sight line of the cinematographer. Referring to Okuzaki as "Sensei", one of the policemen politely asks, "Can you tell us your schedule?" In response, the eccentric veteran outlines his investigation into the murders of Yoshizawa and Nomura. As a result of Okuzaki's incredible self-righteousness, the police once again serve a comic function. He shrewdly uses them to restate his case against Hara Toshio.

As abruptly as they arrived, the officers, seemingly reassured, disappear, and the interview continues. (Surprisingly, the sequestered ex-Sergeant has not taken advantage of their presence to put an end to the confrontation.) Sobbing, Nomura implores the veteran to tell the truth on behalf of his late father. Hara Toshio offers to discuss the matter privately with the relatives. Okuzaki, sensing his purpose undermined, rejects this arrangement. He gestures towards the crew, stating: "If it were the truth, you could say it in front of the camera". Motioning to the photograph on the table, Sakimoto Rinko says: "My brother is here. His spirit. Consider he's here. Speak for him." The accused veteran tries to turn this reference to ancestor worship against her: "If people knew they were executed for desertion, you'd have to bear the shame as their families". Pointing towards the lens, the ex-Sergeant adds, "The camera's rolling. People will see the film and look down on you." Okuzaki refuses this gambit and retorts, similarly motioning to the filmmaker, "They'll think you're hiding the truth". The camera becomes a quiet but expressive witness to the conspiracy of silence. Ultimately, Hara Toshio's resistance falters, and he admits that Privates Yoshizawa and Nomura were shot for desertion well after the war had already ended. Furthermore, the veteran confirms that he was a member of the execution squad, and expresses his deep regrets to Sakimoto and Nomura. The excruciating interview ends with the confession.

Without pause, scene 16 pushes the investigation deeper into the madness of the New Guinea campaign. Okuzaki and the relatives track down ex-medic Hamaguchi Masaichi at a restaurant owned by his family in a shopping mall in Nagata, Kobe. They wander through the mall to find an appropriate place to talk. Once they are seated around a table in the Kotobukiro restaurant, Hamaguchi provides the most dramatic testimony in *The Emperor's Naked Army Marches On*. Finally, after endless denials – in a crucial scene placed at the centre of the film and chillingly set in an elegant restaurant – one of the accused veterans answers questions without equivocation. The viewer's worst fears are confirmed. Speaking of captured Allied soldiers and New Guinea natives, Hamaguchi admits, "We had to eat them to survive. We could be as brutal as that. Men are horrible." The revelations of cannibalism fulfil a cathartic function for veterans, victims, relatives and viewers. Contradicting Sakimoto's line of questioning, however, Hamaguchi denies that Japanese privates, such as Yoshizawa and Nomura, were eaten.

In Hyogo, in scene 17, Okuzaki and the relatives encounter ex-doctor Maruyama Tarō. With those who acknowledge their responsibility in the executions, such as Maruyama, the interviews remain cordial. The ex-Sergeant concludes: "After all, I think Koshimizu was to blame". In scene 18, Nomura and Sakimoto visit the graves of their brothers without Okuzaki. Their comments are pieced together through a series of jump cuts. Framed sitting side-by-side in the cemetery, they summarise the results of their inquiry:

> Sakimoto: They talk different. All different stories. So I think they were all lying.
> Nomura: Our brothers were executed for something they didn't do. They were killed just because the officers wanted to cannibalise them to survive.
> Sakimoto: I think so, too. I think privates were the first to be sacrificed for officers to survive. The area was four square kilometres. No food supply. The easiest way to eat was to prey on low-ranking soldiers. The weakest fell victim first. The officers survived that way.

Seemingly satisfied or simply fed up with the tangle of lies and half-truths, the relatives abandon their investigation, as an intertitle notes: "The two never accompanied Okuzaki again".

On the phone with ex-Sergeant Kojima Shichirō in scene 19, Okuzaki redoubles his efforts to bring ex-Captain Koshimizu to justice, even without the cooperation of the relatives. The sequence reaffirms Okuzaki's dogged pursuit of the guilty. Of the unrepentant ex-Captain, Kojima flatly states, "He deserves death". As the camera pans down from Okuzaki's face to the telephone wiretap and the tape recorder in the foreground, Kojima adds, "As the war ended, no one should be punished for desertion". *The Emperor's Naked Army*

Marches On exhibits some of the paraphernalia of detection – tape recorders, newspaper headlines – common in investigative documentaries such as Errol Morris' *The Thin Blue Line* (1988) and Michael Apted's *Incident at Oglala* (1991).

For the inevitable confrontation with Koshimizu, Okuzaki had hoped to have the assistance of the two relatives. In scene 20, he explains how hard he tried to convince Nomura, Jinpei's brother, to come with him. Not to be undone by their refusal to accompany him on further interviews, Okuzaki simply recruits his own wife and a teacher, Kuwata Hiroshi, for the encounter with the ex-Captain. Smiling, the veteran laughs when he tells Shizumi, "Today you'll be acting not as my wife but as Yoshizawa's sister. You're the relatives of the two victims. Act well. Let me do the talking." Okuzaki appears to appreciate not only the deception involved, but also the understanding implicit in his remark that, under ordinary circumstances, Shizumi *acts* as his wife. Scene 22, therefore, reintroduces a comic note in the grim progression of Okuzaki's investigation and its sordid revelations. As usual in *The Emperor's Naked Army Marches On*, the humour carries a sharp edge. Even more than his decision to resort to violence, this use of deceit undermines the viewer's confidence in Okuzaki. How can he demand complete honesty from the other veterans when he himself is not above lying on behalf of his cause?

Whereas Okuzaki seems religiously attached to literal facts in his investigation, he reveals himself as an opportunist in his search, willing to stage certain actions in his pursuit of the truth. In scene 24, Okuzaki gets support from another opponent of the emperor system, admitting, "I asked Mr Oshima to act as the victim's brother. I think his appearance will make the ex-Sergeant talk." These scenes mirror Hara's collaborative method of documentary filmmaking in which characters perform their lives – and others – for the camera. This casting also substantiates Okuzaki's assertion that he is the author of the film. The knowledge that the so-called relatives are merely stand-ins complicates the viewer's reactions to the encounters that follow. The distinctions between documentary and fiction are effectively blurred.

Together with his wife and Mr Kuwata, Okuzaki confronts Koshimizu Masao at his house in Ohtake, Hiroshima. Scene 21 provides the first glimpse of the man who ordered the murders, although the ex-Captain refuses to shoulder any guilt, "You may blame me, but I'm not ashamed of myself". Although he admits to having authorised the executions, Koshimizu, too, claims that he was under orders from his superior officers, and furthermore that he was not there when the shootings took place. Okuzaki's subsequent frenzied accusations – including his inflammatory comment that "The most cowardly man in Japan is the Emperor. You're loyal to him, like other officers" – fail to perturb the elderly veteran. This interview ends without any meaningful resolution.

A relentless narrative momentum builds over the last third of the documentary. The next scene, 22, takes place the "following day at five in the morning", according to an intertitle. Once again, Okuzaki ambushes Seo Yukio at his home. This time, shaken by the presence of the fake relatives, the ex-Sergeant capitulates and admits his participation in the killings, providing a gruelling account of the shootings. "Death should be instantaneous", Seo comments, his face flushed with tears. "I aimed at the heart of one of them. But they didn't die instantly. Koshimizu shot them with his gun, so they wouldn't suffer any longer." Using a handful of oranges from a basket on the table, the two veterans meticulously reconstruct the relative positions of the firing squad, the victims and the Captain. Overcome with emotion, Seo apologises to Okuzaki's companions. Scene 23 takes place, as another intertitle states, at "2.00 pm the same day". Okuzaki again confronts Takami Minoru at his home. This encounter prolongs the catharsis of the previous scene, as the ex-Sergeant confesses and begs forgiveness. "I'm sorry for what happened today. I apologise", Takami says, bowing deeply to the so-called relatives. "I understand why you are doing this. I'm ashamed of myself. I have done nothing for the victims, or their families. I'm sorry."

These moving confessions fail to satisfy Okuzaki's extraordinary appetite for justice. In the following scene, he calls upon Ōshima Eizaburo to impersonate the brother of another dead soldier, Hashimoto Giichi. According to Okuzaki's jumbled summary, Hashimoto was murdered when five starving soldiers drew lots to decide who among them would be killed and eaten by the others. In the subsequent encounter with Yamada Kichitarō – at 22 minutes by far the longest scene in the film – Okuzaki provides an explicit rationale for his protests: "To reveal the misery of the war will keep the world free from war. They killed a man but reported that he died from disease. The world doesn't know the real face of war." In the ensuing mêlée, Okuzaki kicks the ex-Sergeant repeatedly. Yamada says angrily to the filmmaker behind the camera, "You forgot I helped you", to which his wife replies, "Don't blame them." Eventually Okuzaki himself, having earlier phoned the police, calls for medical assistance for Yamada and the scene ends with the departure of the injured veteran in an ambulance.

Scene 26 shows Okuzaki and his wife standing in front of the hospital. After thanking Shizumi for restraining him, thereby sparing Yamada greater injury from his assault, Okuzaki reasserts the appropriateness of his methods: "Mr Yamada's son-in-law told me that I must not hurt people. But if the result is good, violence is justified. So as long as I live I'll use violence, if it brings good results to me and mankind, by my judgment and my responsibility." After a brief scene in which Okuzaki again prays to console the souls of his dead comrades, and an intertitle which mentions the trip to New Guinea and the seizure of the footage shot there, the unstable veteran proves true to his promise of violence.

The sound of gunfire follows a brief flashback to a shot of Koshimizu. A quick montage of newspaper headlines and articles, dramatically spotlighted, details the protagonist's final direct action: "Attempted Murder!", "Ex-Officer's Son Wounded", "Okuzaki Kenzō", "Victim Seriously Wounded", "Criminal At Large", "His Superior Officer's Son", "'The Son Will Do!'", "Wanted Okuzaki Kenzō" and "Okuzaki Apprehended in Kobe". Even behind bars, the elderly veteran continues to issue pronouncements on his activities. In the next scene, Okuzaki's wife, Shizumi, announces her husband's intentions over the loudspeaker of the sound-truck:

> In order to prove divine punishment, he wanted to kill Koshimizu. He told the plan to his friends. He carried it out on December 15. But he couldn't kill Koshimizu. Instead, he shot Koshimizu's son. But the son didn't die. He thought it was Providence. In the police station cell, he shed tears of gratitude three times. He wants Koshimizu to tell in court about the murder he committed in the Army. His testimony will console the dead and help prevent the breakout of another war.

The Emperor's Naked Army Marches On moves inexorably towards its violent conclusion. The director does not disclose that the attempted assassination took place some nine months after the principal location filming was finished. As depicted, it appears that Okuzaki goes immediately from his confrontation with Yamada to the murder attempt. The sequence of the newspaper headlines echoes the convictions listed at the opening of the documentary, answering the implicit question set up at the beginning. After a series of direct actions, the veteran has returned to prison, convicted of attempted manslaughter, as the final intertitle states: "January 28, 1987 Okuzaki was sentenced to 12 years at hard labour".

Reception history: Japanese memories of the war

The Emperor's Naked Army Marches On provoked substantial controversy when it was released in Japan in 1987.[59] Commercial distributors refused to handle the film, fearing it would trigger attacks from violent right-wing protesters. Hara remembers meeting with executives in the film industry:

> I was wondering if some of the large companies, like Iwanami, Shōchiku, Tōhō, or Seibu, would show it. I went to meet their representatives. For example, the Shōchiku people told me that they would like to show the film, but if they did the right-wing would visit them, that they would protest with their sound-trucks in front of the theaters. They all said the same thing – 'we'd like to show it, but we can't.'[60]

During the early months of 1987, the film was screened in public halls in Tokyo for short runs of several days. Word-of-mouth publicity and a torrent of positive reviews sparked audience interest. In August, an 80-seat art theatre in Tokyo, Yurosupesu (Eurospace), began showing the film. It played there for three months, filling the theatre daily with standing-room-only crowds. Eventually, it was shown in most cities in Japan and released on video, reaching an audience estimated at one million. In spite of being rejected by mainstream distributors, *The Emperor's Naked Army Marches On* came to enjoy considerable commercial success for a non-fiction film.

Okuzaki's political views defy easy classification, and this resulted in some unexpected responses to the documentary. While many, including the director, were convinced that *The Emperor's*

Naked Army Marches On would draw the anger of extremist groups, a few right-wing activists apparently found a kindred spirit in Okuzaki. As Hara recalled, "[m]embers of a right-wing group came to see the film in Kyoto in autumn 1987. The film was shown in a hall for about three days. I was told that when the right-wing members emerged from the film, they were afraid. I was told that they bought Okuzaki's book, and said they understood his feelings."[61] The reactions of political parties and official government agencies to the film were also somewhat unpredictable. The taciturn Imperial Household Agency, while keenly aware of it, withheld comment. The conservative Liberal Democratic Party, whose representatives had been targets for assassination by Okuzaki, also chose to ignore the scandalous documentary. Newspapers affiliated with the Nihon Shakaitō (Japan Socialist Party) recommended the work. But it was the reaction of the Japan Communist Party that surprised most people, including the director. While the Japan Communist Party has been a long-time critic of the monarchy – and especially of the Shōwa Emperor's role in the Pacific War – nevertheless, the party's newspaper, *Akahata*, criticised *The Emperor's Naked Army Marches On*.[62]

The reception of the film, therefore, was as diverse and complicated as the documentary itself. Film critics who recommended the work were nevertheless faced with the problem of what to call it. Was it, in fact, a documentary? If so, what type of documentary? Or was it better to call it a dramatic film?[63] Hara could not have been more pleased with the confusion, for his goal has long been to make "action documentaries" that call into question clear genre distinctions. The director energetically joined the debate about his work, demonstrating a forthrightness rare for producers. His first essay on the film appeared in the June 1987 issue of *Imeji foramu*, a leading Japanese film journal. This created a stir which led to further debate. Later that year, Shissō Productions published a transcript of the finished film, along with Hara's 119-page account of the making of the documentary.[64]

The Emperor's Naked Army Marches On raised – and still raises – numerous issues for intellectuals, from the legitimacy of Okuzaki's indictment of the Shōwa Emperor to the question of historical memory. There is also the problem of Okuzaki's methods. Does the seriousness of the crimes committed in New Guinea justify Okuzaki's own use of violence and disregard for the law in the context of democratic Japan in the 1980s? The historian Akira Iriye felt that Okuzaki's extremism mirrored that of the Japanese military:

> His fanaticism – at one point he says, 'the use of violence is justified for the good of mankind' – is reminiscent of Japanese wartime behavior, and it is possible to see in his facial expressions, stripped of surface civilities, the same combination of brutality and self-righteousness that impressed foreign observers of the Japanese army during the war.[65]

In making the documentary, Hara had hoped to capture how militarist values survived in his parents' generation 40 years after the Pacific War. Ironically for Iriye, these tendencies seem to persist in Okuzaki as much as, if not more so, in the other veterans. The anti-war crusader is, after all, the only soldier in his own "divine army". In a rebuttal to a reviewer who described his feelings for the eccentric protagonist as 10% empathy and 90% disgust, literary critic Karatani Kōjin suggested 100% sympathy for Okuzaki as the proper response. The imprisoned veteran later cited Karatani's off-the-cuff comment as the correct reading of the documentary.[66]

One concern which intellectuals shared with film critics was the question of ethics in non-fiction filmmaking. Should not the director have put down the camera and interceded in situations where some restraint on Okuzaki seemed necessary? Hara has been asked this question many times:

> Maybe I should have intervened. It was really a case by case decision. He wasn't killing anybody, just scuffling. You know, when we were filming, we never knew what Okuzaki was going to do. He is frightening. Remember when Okuzaki attacked Yamada, the old man, that was frightening. I had a little feeling that I should stop filming. But within the minds of movie makers, there is a feeling that the filming must go on, when one is behind the camera, you know. If I had not been holding the camera, it might have been another story. A person with a camera thinks he must film.[67]

Another disturbing question remains about *The Emperor's Naked Army Marches On*. If Okuzaki had not been the subject of the film, would he still have shot Koshimizu's son, who committed no crime? Did the making of the documentary contribute to the wounding of an innocent man? Hara only inflamed the argument by candidly admitting that he considered filming the murder attempt after Okuzaki proposed it.[68] Disturbed by his own morbid curiosity, Hara has asked himself: "Is film God for me?"[69]

Hara's confession and the debate it sparked formed only one of the stories that developed parallel to the film's popularity. In the same year that *The Emperor's Naked Army Marches On* was released, Okuzaki's trial was completed, and his appeal worked its way through the Japanese judicial system. His trial ended in January 1987, with a sentence of twelve years' hard labour for attempted manslaughter. (Hara edited this verdict into the end of the film shortly before public showings began.) Okuzaki immediately appealed against the decision, and his lawyer introduced *The Emperor's Naked Army Marches On* to the Hiroshima Court of Appeals as evidence. The presiding judge agreed that a video of the film could be shown as part of the appeal, spurring Hara to quickly produce one. On 4 September 1987, the defendant, several lawyers, three magistrates and an additional twenty spectators sat down in the courtroom for a viewing. Film reviewer Matsuda Masao noted that the judges took the best seats for themselves and remained spellbound for two hours.[70] This was also the first time the imprisoned veteran saw the film. The screening did not help Okuzaki's case, however, as the higher court upheld the lower court's ruling.

While benefiting from unusual publicity when first released, the film owes its popularity to its startling subject-matter and engaging protagonist. Many found the elderly veteran one of the most thrilling and exotic characters they had ever encountered in a film, fiction or documentary. Okuzaki's unorthodox methods and the unsavoury memories he churned up even produced a feeling of physical shock in some reviewers. The renowned film critic, Satō Tadao – who began his review of *The Emperor's Naked Army Marches On* with the simple statement, "This is an incredible film!" – admitted that after seeing the documentary he felt as though he had been struck a blow.[71]

For Japanese viewers, the most inflammatory part of the film – even more than the confessions of cannibalism – was Okuzaki's stubborn insistence on condemning the Shōwa Emperor as a coward for refusing to accept responsibility for the war. None of Hara's controversial films has been shown on television in Japan,[72] and Hara explained in 1992 why *The Emperor's Naked Army Marches On*, in particular, will likely never be broadcast: "Because it is a film about the emperor system, about Okuzaki, a movie about the man who shot *pachinko* balls at the Emperor".[73] Unlike scholarly essays printed in journals with limited circulation, *The Emperor's Naked Army Marches On* provided an accessible and entertaining indictment of the Shōwa Emperor as a war criminal. Reactions to this indictment ranged from distaste to delight. Viewers from the war generation were generally stunned by the film, shocked by the audacity of Okuzaki's actions. Many young Japanese, less supportive of official attempts to regulate the dignity of the Imperial House, were probably thrilled to watch a film that contradicted all they had been told about the Emperor.

When *The Emperor's Naked Army Marches On* was released in 1987, most Japanese – including the Japanese government – still had not undertaken the soul-searching about the war often said to characterise German *Vergangenheitsbewältigung*, the attempt to come to terms with the Nazi era,[74] or even similar efforts by the French, beginning in the 1970s, to address the tangled history of the Vichy period (1940-44). Selective memory of the Pacific War continued to shift attention away from the brutality of Japan's imperialist expansion. Many Japanese saw themselves exclusively as victims of the war, a phenomenon which historians refer to as *higaisha ishiki* (victims' consciousness). In 1945, after all, the Allied forces, led by the American military, waged a bombing campaign against civilian targets that concluded with the atomic destruction of Hiroshima and Nagasaki. The suffering experienced when the conflict was brought home to Japan displaced memories of Japanese aggression. After the war, Japanese people preferred to identify with the civilian victims of the A-bombs, rather than with their own soldiers who committed atrocities all across Asia. Similarly, the myth of the Shōwa Emperor's pacifist nature remained intact until the late-1980s, when a variety of factors, including *The Emperor's Naked Army Marches On*, strongly questioned it.[75]

In sum, *The Emperor's Naked Army Marches On* was controversial precisely because it subverted official attempts to gloss over Japan's responsibility for the conflict. The documentary rejects the notion that the Japanese were only victims. It leaves the Imperial Military no dignity and offers no justification for the war. The film belittles the concept of a national community officially engaged in a heroic war to free Asia from Western imperialism. Starving in New Guinea, Japanese soldiers cannot catch the natives whom they have liberated, so they are reduced to cannibalising each other.

The reception of *The Emperor's Naked Army Marches On* bears comparison to reactions in France to Marcel Ophüls' epic documentary about the Vichy era, *Le Chagrin et la pitié* (*The Sorrow and the Pity*, 1971). State-controlled stations in France declined to broadcast Ophüls' film, although it was produced with funds from European Television. Instead, *The Sorrow and the Pity* opened in a small art theatre in the Latin Quarter in Paris, gradually reaching a sizeable audience in the capital. The documentary offended almost all of the established power blocs in France; the Communist Party complained that their contribution to the Resistance was under-emphasised, while the Gaullists felt that simply raising the issue of collaboration was "unpatriotic".[76] In the aftermath of the 1968 uprisings, however, a substantial audience of students, disaffected workers and intellectuals appreciated Ophüls' film because it overturned accepted versions of French history. The 3½-hour documentary – through brilliant juxtaposition of interviews and archival footage – shattered the myth of a unified French Resistance fighting to the last against the German occupation, and at the same time raised the issue of French complicity in the Holocaust.[77] As the historian Henry Rousso shows in *The Vichy Syndrome: History and Memory in France since 1944*, Ophüls' work had a tremendous impact on the historical image of France during the Nazi occupation, encouraging fiction filmmakers of the 1970s to look back on the dark years of the war.[78]

Like popular films in France that glorify the Resistance, postwar features in Japan often portray the Japanese as helpless victims of the war. Films condemn the horrific atomic bombings but provide no context, leaving the viewer with the impression that the Fifteen Years War began in August 1945, instead of in 1931 when Japan first began aggressively to expand its empire in China. Recent films by Kurosawa and Imamura have reinforced this image of the Japanese as victims, by focusing exclusively on the atomic bombings and the aftermath of the destruction. Both *Hachigatsu no kyōshikyoku* (*Rhapsody in August*, 1991) and *Kuroi ame* (*Black Rain*, 1988) tell of the lingering effects of the bomb on families in the postwar period. Kurosawa's film, in particular, was criticised in Japan for reinforcing the victims' consciousness. One of the few recent features that looks at wartime atrocities committed by Japanese authorities, Kumai Kei's *Sea and Poison*, lists Hara as an assistant director. Kumai's film details medical experiments on prisoners of war performed under military supervision at Kyushu Imperial University in spring 1945.

The Emperor's Naked Army Marches On marks a breach in representations of wartime Japan. By chronicling the activities of a protester who attacks the status quo, it remains one of the lone voices challenging established myths about the war years. Hara's film indicts the Shōwa Emperor, and both Hara and Kobayashi, the producer, have expressed their desire to tell a different history of the era. After the film's release, Kobayashi remarked: "I feel angry that we are not informed what exactly happened in the war. And the ministries and those concerned are reluctant to give information. When I think of the feelings of the people of Asia, I regret very much to see too many movies which praise the war."[79] The current crisis in the Japanese film industry may conspire to keep others from re-examining the conflict in the light of recent revelations.[80] Like Ophüls' landmark film, however, Hara Kazuo's brilliant documentary, *The Emperor's Naked Army Marches On*, may embolden other directors to confront the sorrow and the terror of Japan's activities during the Second World War.

Notes

1. Hirano Kyoko, "*The Japanese Tragedy*: Film Censorship and the American Occupation", *Radical History Review* 41 (1988): 67-92.

2. Kenneth J Ruoff and Jeffrey K Ruoff, "Japan's Outlaw Filmmaker: An Interview with Hara Kazuo", *Iris: A Journal of Theory on Image and Sound* 16 (spring 1993): 104.

3. Ibid: 107.

4. Ibid: 106.

5. Ibid: 107.

6. Ibid: 113.

7. Several essays are collected in Shissō purodakushon (ed), *Sayonara CP* (Tokyo: Shissō purodakushon, 1972).

8. According to Kobayashi Sachiko, in an interview with Kenneth Ruoff on 10 May 1992, *Sayonara CP* cost about 1 500 000 yen (or $15 000 at 100 yen to the dollar).

9. See, for example, Kobayashi Sachiko, "Atte mo ii sonzai nan da", *Brīn* May 1973: 5; and Hara Kazuo, "Shintai no kaihō ni koso", *Gendai tenbō* July 1973: 168-173.

10. Jeffrey K Ruoff, "Family Programming, Television, and American Culture: A Case Study of *An American Family*" (PhD dissertation, Department of Communication Studies, University of Iowa, Iowa City, 1995).

11. Ruoff and Ruoff: 112.

12. Ibid.

13. Jeffrey K Ruoff, "Home Movies of the Avant-Garde: Jonas Mekas and the New York Art World", *Cinema Journal* 30: 3 (spring 1991): 18. Mekas' experimental film received significant commentary when shown in Tokyo in 1973, and critics later discussed *Extreme Private Eros: Love Song 1974* in relation to

Mekas' autobiographical journey to his native land.

14 Ruoff and Ruoff: 108.

15 Jay Ruby, "Ethnography as Trompe L'Œil: Film and Anthropology", in Jay Ruby (ed), *A Crack in the Mirror: Reflexive Perspectives in Anthropology* (Philadelphia: University of Pennsylvania Press, 1982): 130.

16 Ruoff and Ruoff: 108.

17 "Tennō ga 'sengo shori' ni iyoku", *Sentaku* December 1992: 121.

18 "Tennō hatsugen e no Nihonjin 20-nin no iken", *Shūkan asahi* 10 October 1975: 18.

19 Haruko Taya Cook and Theodore F Cook, *Japan at War: An Oral History* (New York: The New Press, 1992): 277. *Japan at War* was published five years after the release of *The Emperor's Naked Army Marches On*. The eyewitness accounts in the book echo and confirm the horrifying testimonies given in the film. For example, Ogawa Masatsugu, a veteran of the New Guinea campaign, recalls his fear of being preyed upon by fellow Japanese soldiers: "Near the end we were told not to go out alone to get water, even in daytime. We could trust the men we knew, but there were rumors that you could never be sure what would happen if another of our own soldiers came upon you." (273).

20 Ibid: 363.

21 Ibid: 376.

22 The term was made famous by Studs Terkel's *"The Good War": An Oral History of World War Two* (London: Hamish Hamilton, 1985).

23 The adviser was Kido Kōichi, who held the office of Lord Keeper of the Privy Seal. Quoted in Daikichi Irokawa, *The Age of Hirohito: In Search of Modern Japan*, translated by Mikiso

24 Mizuno Yasuji, "'Tennō goke ni taisuru bōkō'-han to no gokūchu kaikenki", *Josei jishin* 12 December 1969: 50.

25 Cook and Cook: 267.

26 For estimates of the number of war dead on all sides, see John W Dower, *War Without Mercy: Race and Power in the Pacific War* (New York: Pantheon Books, 1986): 293-317.

27 15 August 1945, radio address to the nation. Quoted in Herbert Bix, "The Shōwa Emperor's 'Monologue' and the Problem of War Responsibility", *Journal of Japanese Studies* 18: 2 (summer 1992): 302.

28 For a contemporary translation of Higashikuni's address, see "Premier Prince Naruhiko Higashi-kuni's Address at the Eighty-Eighth Session of the Diet, September 5, 1945", *Contemporary Japan* (April-December 1945): 280-288.

29 Reprinted in *Jurisuto* 938 (15 July 1989): 176. The report focuses on the decision to attack the United States in 1941, and does not address Japan's military actions against China and other Asian countries.

30 For a study of the Emperor's tours, see Sakamoto Kōjirō, *Shōchō tennōsei e no pafomansu* (Tokyo: Yamakawa shuppansha, 1989). The Emperor was welcomed by crowds of supporters on virtually all of his trips.

31 After the Shōwa Emperor died in 1989, numerous documents were released that shed new light on his pre-war and wartime political role. These sources show that the Emperor, far more often than the orthodox interpretation suggested, was a hands-on monarch. Bix and Irokawa, both cited above, employ these new sources to criticise the political role of the Shōwa Emperor.

32 Yamada Kazuo, "Nihon eigashi no naka no tennō", *Sōtokushū: Tennōsei o tou* (Tokyo: Bunka hyōron, 1986): 354-364.

33   This exchange between two of Japan's famous postwar prime ministers took place in the Budget Committee of the Lower House of the Diet on 31 January 1952. See *Daijūsankai kokkai shūgiin yosan iinkai gijiroku* 5: 19. It also appears in Watanabe Osamu, *Sengo seijishi no naka no tennōsei* (Tokyo: Aoki shoten, 1990): 209-210. Nakasone was a nationalist even when it was unfashionable to take pride in being Japanese. Elected to the House of Representatives in 1947, Nakasone wore black ties in the Diet to express his mournful feelings about the foreign occupation of his country. He was chastised by American authorities for flying the banned Japanese flag in front of his house.

34   For one example of Prime Minister Nakasone, in the Diet, defending the Shōwa Emperor's role in the war, see *Daihyakuyonkai kokkai shūgiin yosan iinkai giroku* 20 (8 March 1986): 32-34.

35   Mizuno: 50.

36   Okuzaki Kenzō, *Hikokumin Okuzaki Kenzō wa uttaeru* (Tokyo: Shinsensha, 1987).

37   "Kyūn to tennōsama o neratta tama ga", *Josei jishin* 13 January 1969: 24.

38   Ruoff and Ruoff: 107.

39   Ibid: 110. This chronicle of the making of *The Emperor's Naked Army Marches On* draws extensively from our published interview with the director in *Iris*, as well as from Hara's own account, "Seisaku nōto", in Hara Kazuo and Shissō purodakushon (eds), *Yukiyukite shingun seisaku nōto* (Tokyo: Shissō purodakushon, 1987): 3-122.

40   Dower (43) writes: "[I]t was in 1937, with the Rape of Nanking, that the killing of noncombatants escalated to a massive scale. Nanking fell on December 12 after heavy shelling and bombing, and for the next six weeks Japanese troops engaged in the widespread execution, rape, and random murder of Chinese men and women both in the captured city and outlying communities. The total number of Chinese killed is

controversial, but a middle-range estimate puts the combined deaths from both the shelling and subsequent atrocities at two hundred thousand."

[41] Ruoff and Ruoff: 105.

[42] Ibid: 109.

[43] Okuzaki Kenzō, "Yukiyukite shingun o mita shujinkō no kansō", *Kinema junpō* 1 December 1987, reprinted in Matsuda Masao and Takahashi Taketomo (eds), *Gunron yukiyukite shingun* (Tokyo: Tōgosha, 1988): 353-365.

[44] Hara (1987): 120.

[45] Ibid: 47.

[46] Ruoff and Ruoff: 109.

[47] Hara (1987): 47.

[48] Ruoff and Ruoff: 108.

[49] François Niney, "*L'armée de l'empereur s'avance*", *Cahiers du Cinéma* 406 (1988): 41.

[50] Ruoff and Ruoff: 108.

[51] Ibid: 112. Emphasis in original.

[52] John G Cawelti, "*Chinatown* and Generic Transformation in Recent American Films", in Gerald Mast, Marshall Cohen and Leo Braudy (eds), *Film Theory and Criticism: Introductory Readings*, fourth edition (New York; Oxford: Oxford University Press, 1992): 499.

[53] Kurosawa Akira's *Rashomon* (1950), adapted from two stories by Akutagawa Ryūnosuke, recounts the events of a rape and murder from the separate perspectives of four characters. "The audience is left with the feeling of the essential relativity of truth", in the words of Joseph L Anderson and Donald Richie,

The Japanese Film: Art and Industry (New York: Grove Press, 1960): 224.

54 Ruoff and Ruoff: 110.

55 Bill Nichols, *Representing Reality: Issues and Concepts in Documentary* (Bloomington; Indianapolis: Indiana University Press, 1991): 3-4.

56 Claude Lanzmann, "From the Holocaust to the *Holocaust*", *Telos* (autumn/winter 1980): 41.

57 For a more scholarly approach to this issue, see Benedict Anderson, *Imagined Communities: Reflections on the Origin and Spread of Nationalism* (London: Verso, 1991).

58 For a detailed discussion of Ozu's camera style, see David Bordwell, *Ozu and the Poetics of Cinema* (Princeton: Princeton University Press, 1988): 84.

59 For a collection of 55 essays about the film, see Matsuda and Takahashi (eds).

60 Ruoff and Ruoff: 111.

61 Ibid.

62 Ibid.

63 Kuroko Kazuo, among other reviewers, addressed this issue. See Kuroko, "'Nichijō' o utsu shingun, soshite hitotsu no wadakamari", in Matsuda and Takahashi (eds): 23-32.

64 Hara (1987): 3-122.

65 Akira Iriye, "The Emperor's Naked Army Marches On", *The American Historical Review* 94: 4 (October 1989): 1037.

66 On 14 March 1992, Karatani Kōjin lectured on the films of Hara Kazuo – and, in particular, reactions to *The Emperor's Naked Army Marches On* – at a conference entitled "Image Theory, Image Culture, and Contemporary Japan", hosted by

the Institute for Cinema and Culture at the University of Iowa. Organised by Dudley Andrew and Michael Raine, the conference brought together leading American and Japanese film scholars for four days of presentations and film showings. A fascinating discussion with Hara followed a packed screening of *The Emperor's Naked Army Marches On*. We are grateful to the organisers for bringing the director to Iowa City and for encouraging us to write about his work.

[67] Ruoff and Ruoff: 109.

[68] Hara (1987): 50-51.

[69] Ibid: 120.

[70] Matsuda Masao, "Okuzaki saiban wocchingu", in Matsuda and Takahashi (eds): 336.

[71] Satō Tadao, "Kore wa monosugoi eiga de aru", in Matsuda and Takahashi (eds): 205. Satō's review originally appeared in *Kinema junpō*, March 1987 (end of month issue).

[72] Kobayashi Sachiko, interview with Kenneth Ruoff, 10 May 1992.

[73] Ruoff and Ruoff: 107. According to Hara, television executives feared the consequences of broadcasting such a contentious work to a national audience. Similarly, in 1989, the distributor of Bernardo Bertolucci's *The Last Emperor* (1988), Shōchiku-Fuji, removed archival footage of Japanese military atrocities in China from the version released in Japan. See Keiko McDonald, "Japan", in John A Lent, *The Asian Film Industry* (Austin: University of Texas Press, 1990): 50-51.

[74] On the topic of *Vergangenheitsbewältigung* ("working through, or coming to terms with, the past"), see Alexander Mitscherlich and Margarete Mitscherlich, *The Inability to Mourn: Principles of Collective Behavior* (New York: Grove Press, 1975).

[75] The protracted illness of the Emperor, and his death in 1989, led to a reappraisal of the war years. See Norma Field, *In the Realm of a Dying Emperor* (New York: Pantheon Books, 1991).

76 Stanley Hoffmann, "In the Looking Glass", in Mireille Johnston (ed), *The Sorrow and the Pity: A film by Marcel Ophuls* (New York: Outerbridge and Lazard, 1972): xiii.

77 General Charles De Gaulle, France's pre-eminent postwar figure, established the myth of unified resistance to close the Vichy era. Henry Rousso has traced its origin to De Gaulle's speech on 25 August 1944, announcing the liberation of Paris from the Nazis: "Paris! Paris humiliated! Paris broken! Paris martyrized! But Paris liberated! Liberated by itself, by its own people with the help of the armies of France, with the support and aid of France as a whole, of fighting France, of the only France, of the true France, of eternal France." Quoted in Henry Rousso, *The Vichy Syndrome: History and Memory in France since 1944*, translated by Arthur Goldhammer (Cambridge, MA; London: Harvard University Press, 1991): 16. In seeking to resurrect *la gloire de France*, De Gaulle not only exaggerated the French role in the liberation, but, more importantly, ignored active French collaboration with the Nazis in the deportation of French Jews and other unflattering details of the occupation years. *The Sorrow and the Pity* was released one year after *le Général* died.

78 Rousso: 100-114.

79 Quoted in Makiko Ogihara, "The Emperor's Naked Army Marches On", *The Japan Times* 4 August 1987: 11.

80 For more information on the structural transformation of the Japanese film industry in the 1980s, see McDonald.

Credits

original title	Yukiyukite shingun
English title	The Emperor's Naked Army Marches On
country of production	Japan
year of production	1987
length	122 minutes
gauge	35mm / 16mm
producer	Kobayashi Sachiko
production company	Shissō Productions
director	Hara Kazuo
cinematographer	Hara Kazuo
editor	Nabeshima Jun
cast	(see page vi)

Index

36th Engineering Corps
    11, 15, 17, 30

Akahata (newspaper)   39
Akira, Iriye   40
Akutagawa, Ryūnosuke   49n53
American Family, An   6
Apted, Michael   35
Baka ni sunna (exhibition of photographs)   4
Bertolucci, Bernardo   51n73
Black Rain see *Kuroi ame*
Buckner, Noel   25
Buta to gunkan (Pigs and Battleships)   6
Cahiers du Cinéma   18
Cawelti, John G   23
Chagrin et la pitié, Le (The Sorrow and the Pity)   43
Children of the Sun, The see *Taiyō no ko*
Choy, Christine   8
Cook, Haruko Taya   10
Cook, Theodore F   10
De Gaulle, Charles   52n77
Dedicated Life, A see *Zenshin shōsetsuka*
Directors' Guild of Japan   18
Dore, Mary   25
Eijanaika   8, 14

Extreme Private Eros: Love Song 1974 see *Kyokushiteki erosu koiuta 1974*
Eyes on the Prize   25
Far East International Military Tribunal   11
Field, Connie   25
Fifteen Years War   4, 43
Fires on the Plains see *Nobi*
French Communist Party   43
Fukūshu suru wa ware ni ari (Vengeance is Mine)   8, 14
Gilbert, Craig   6
Good Fight, The   25
Goodbye CP see *Sayonara CP*
Hachigatsu no kyōshikyoku (Rhapsody in August)   43
Hamaguchi, Masaichi
    16, 19, 31, 33, 34
Hampton, Henry   25
Haneda Airport, Tokyo   9
Hara, Toshio   31-33
Hashimoto, Giichi   36
Hirohito, Emperor
    2, 3, 9-13, 19-22, 25, 27, 28, 32, 36, 39, 42, 44
Hiroshima
    11, 23, 25, 30, 35, 42
Hiroshima Court of Appeals   41
Hiroshima, mon amour   23

Hiroshima Prison 16, 26
History of Japan as Told by a Bar Hostess see *Nippon sengoshi: Madamu Onboro no seikatsu*
Hollywood 19
Holocaust 25, 43
Hyogo Police 21, 23, 28
Ichikawa, Kon 2
Ikimono no kiroku (Record of a Living Being) 23
Imamura, Shōhei 3, 6, 8, 9, 14, 16, 43
Imeji foramu (journal) 39
Imperial House 13, 42
Imperial Household Agency 12, 39
Imperial Palace 3
Imperial Rescript 10
Incident at Oglala 35
Indonesian Consulate, Kobe 17
Inoue, Mitsuharu 4, 8, 9
Isawa Police 32
Iwanami 38
Japan at War: An Oral History (book) 10
Japan Communist Party see Nihon Kyōsantō
Japan Socialist Party see Nihon Shakaitō
Japan's Longest Day see *Nihon no ichiban nagai hi*
Japanese Tragedy, The see *Nippon no higeki*
Jiyū Minshutō (Liberal Democratic Party) 17, 39
Karatani, Kōjin 18, 40

Karayuki-san (Karayuki-san, the Making of a Prostitute) 3
Kawakita Memorial Film Institute 18
Kido, Kōichi 46n23
Kobayashi, Sachiko 4-7, 14, 16, 44, 45n8
Kobe Prison 24, 28
Kobe University 27
Kojima, Kiyofumi 10
Kojima, Shichirō 34
Koshimizu, Masao 16, 26, 29, 30, 34-37, 41
Kumai, Kei 8, 44
Kuroi ame (Black Rain) 43
Kurosawa, Akira 23, 43, 44, 49n53
Kuwata, Hiroshi 35
Kyokushiteki erosu koiuta 1974 (Extreme Private Eros: Love Song 1974) 6-8
Kyushu Imperial University 44
Lanzmann, Claude 25, 26
Last Emperor, The 51n73
Liberal Democratic Party see Jiyū Minshutō
Life and Times of Rosie the Riveter, The 25
Life of Urayama Kirio, The see *Urayama Kirio no shozo*
Makiko, Ogihara 52n79
Maruyama, Tarō 34
Matsuda, Masao 41
Matsuo the Untamed Comes Home see *Muhō Matsu kokyō ni kaeru*
McElwee, Ross 7

Me, a Black see Moi, un noir
Mekas, Jonas 7
Miyagi, Kikuko 10
Moi, un noir (Me, a Black) 8
Morris, Errol 35
Muhō Matsu kokyō ni kaeru (Matsuo the Untamed Comes Home) 14
Museum of Modern Art 8
Nagasaki 11, 14, 42
Nakasone, Yasuhiro 12, 13, 20, 48n33
Nanking Massacre 14, 15, 17
Narita Airport 17
Naruhiko, Higashikuni 11
Nazism 22, 42, 43
New York University 8
Nichols, Bill 25
Nihon Kyōsantō (Japan Communist Party) 20, 39
Nihon no ichiban nagai hi (Japan's Longest Day) 12
Nihon Shakaitō (Japan Socialist Party) 39
Nikkatsu Studios 9
Nikon Salon 4
Nippon no higeki (The Japanese Tragedy) 2
Nippon sengoshi: Madamu Onboro no seikatsu (History of Japan as Told by a Bar Hostess) 3
Nobi (Fires on the Plains) 2
Nomura, Jinpei 29, 31, 33-35
Nomura, Toshiya 31-35
Nuremburg Trials 22
Ogawa, Masatsugu 46n19
Ogawa, Tamotsu 10

Okuzaki, Shizumi 21, 26, 30, 35, 37
Ophüls, Marcel 43, 44
Ōshima, Eizaburo 35, 36
Otagaki, Mr 27
Ōya, Sōichi 12
Ozu, Yasujirō 28
Pearl Harbor 10
Pigs and Battleships see Buta to gunkan
Rashomon 23
Record of a Living Being see Ikimono no kiroku
Reminiscences of a Journey to Lithuania 7
Resnais, Alain 23
Rhapsody in August see Hachigatsu no kyōshikyoku
Rouch, Jean 8
Rousso, Henry 43, 52n77
Saitō, Masaharu 5, 7
Sakimoto, Rinko 31-34
Sano, Miss 27
Satō, Tadao 41
Sayonara CP (Goodbye CP) 5, 6
Sea and Poison see Umi to dokuyaku
Seibu 38
Seo, Yukio 22, 24, 30-32, 36
Sherman's March 7
Shidehara, Kijūrō 12
Shimamoto, Iseko 16, 22, 27, 29
Shimamoto, Masayuki 17
Shissō Productions 5, 14, 39
Shoah 25
Shōchiku 38
Shōchiku-Fuji 51n73

Sills, Sam 25
Sorrow and the Pity, The see Le Chagrin et la pitié
Suzuki, Kantarō 11
Taiyō no ko (The Children of the Sun) 8
Takami, Minoru 15, 22, 23, 26, 29-31, 36
Takeda, Miyuki 6, 7
Tanaka, Kakuei 21, 28
Thin Blue Line, The 35
Tōhō 38
Tōkyō Shashin Senmon Gakkō (Tokyo Academy of Photography) 4
Umi to dokuyaku (Sea and Poison) 8, 44
Urayama, Kirio 8, 9
Urayama Kirio no shozo (The Life of Urayama Kirio) 9
Vengeance is Mine see Fukūshu suru wa ware ni ari
Vichy period 42, 43
Vichy Syndrome: History and Memory in France since 1944, The 43
Waseda University 9
Wewak Garrison 17, 29
Who Killed Vincent Chin? 8
Wiseman, Frederick 26
Yamada, Kichitarō 15, 21-23, 26, 27, 36-38, 40
Yasukuni Shrine 13, 20
Yasuoka, Takuji 16, 17
Yokoi, Shōichi 9
Yokota, Hiroshi 5
Yokota, Yoshiko 5
Yoshida, Shigeru 12, 13

Yoshizawa 29-35
Yurosupesu 38
Zenshin shōsetsuka (A Dedicated Life) 8, 9

Cinetek series

This new series encompasses important films in the history of world cinema. The series aims to be as wide-ranging as possible, and preference is given to neglected, "difficult" or confrontational films. Each book evaluates and analyses a key film, providing a detailed textual reading and a close examination of individual scenes. All books are paperback and 64 pages in length. The following titles are published or in preparation:

Antônio das Mortes
Randal Johnson · 0 948911 10 7

The Asthenic Syndrome
Jane Taubman · 0 948911 33 6

Black Rain
Hector Rodriguez · 0 948911 07 7

Chance of a Lifetime
Alan Burton · 0 948911 56 5

Dead Ringers
Michael Grant · 0 948911 03 4

The Emperor's Naked Army Marches On
Jeffrey Ruoff and Kenneth Ruoff
0 948911 05 0

Fail Safe
Frank R Cunningham
0 948911 42 5

A Funny Dirty Little War
David Foster · 0 948911 06 9

The Human Condition
David Desser · 0 948911 16 6

Jew Süss
Susan Tegel · 0 948911 20 4

The Manchurian Candidate
Stephen Badsey · 0 948911 62 X

Messidor
Jim Leach · 0 948911 01 8

The Navigator
John Downie · 0 948911 65 4

Near Death
Barry Grant · 0 948911 02 6

Occupation in 26 Pictures
Daniel Goulding · 0 948911 64 6

The Official Story
Cynthia Ramsey · 0 948911 08 5

Omar Gatlato
Roy Armes · 0 948911 18 2

A Page of Madness
Aaron Gerow · 0 948911 81 6

Poison
Justin Wyatt · 0 948911 21 2

Red Psalm
Graham Petrie · 0 948911 11 5

Sarraounia
Françoise Pfaff · 0 948911 88 3

Scream from Silence
André Loiselle · 0 948911 32 8

Song of the Exile
George Semsel · 0 948911 15 8

The Spirit of the Beehive
Virginia Higginbotham
0 948911 12 3

Sunless
Jon Kear · 0 948911 37 9